The Migraine Cookbook:

More Than 100 Healthy and Delicious Recipes

**ENDORSED BY
THE MIGRAINE ASSOCIATION
OF CANADA**

COMPILED BY MICHELE SHARP

KEY PORTER BOOKS

Canadian Cataloguing in Publication Data

The migraine cookbook: more than 100 healthy and delicious recipes for
    migraine sufferers.

Includes bibliographical references and index.
ISBN 1-55263-317-9

1. Migraine – Diet therapy – Recipes. I. Sharp, Michele, 1959–

RC392.M53 2001   641.5′631   C2001-930482-X

The publisher gratefully acknowledges the support of the Canada Council for the Arts and
the Ontario Arts Council for its publishing program.

We acknowledge the financial support of the Government of Canada through the Book
Publishing Industry Development Program (BPIDP) for our publishing activities.

Key Porter Books Limited
70 The Esplanade
Toronto, Ontario
Canada M5E 1R2

www.keyporter.com

Electronic formatting: Jean Lightfoot Peters
Design: Peter Maher

Printed and bound in Canada

01 02 03 04 05 06 6 5 4 3 2 1

Contents

Foreword

Migraine is one of the most undertreated, misunderstood and misdiagnosed disorders of the last century. And yet it is a serious medical disorder that significantly affects millions of North Americans. In fact, prevalence studies indicate that 15 to 18 percent of women, 5 to 6 percent of men, 4 to 5 percent of children under twelve, and 10 percent of adolescents suffer from this disorder. As Rosemary Dudley, the founder of The Migraine Association of Canada, stated "Perhaps no other condition so disrupts the lives of its victims and yet evokes so little sympathy and compassion for the afflicted."

As Rosemary's comment suggests, migraine has a significant impact on an individual's personal and professional life. It can lead to lost work days, hindered job performance, restricted activities and disrupted relationships. A recent Statistics Canada report indicates that 7 million work days are lost annually to migraine. Another study in the U.S. estimates that 112 million bedridden days a year costs U.S. employers as much as $13 billion, and the U.S. economy $1 billion in direct medical costs.

While there is no known cure for migraine, understanding your triggers can help you take charge of your attacks. For those of you who find that certain foods can be a trigger, *The Migraine Cookbook* will help to educate and empower you. It has been designed to make you think more about your lifestyle so that you can recognize patterns that lead up to an attack. Through identifying and eliminating or avoiding your triggers, I hope you will be able to provide yourself a measure of relief against the terrible pain of migraine.

The inspiration for this book must go first to our Fredericton, New Brunswick chapter. They were a wonderful source for many of the delicious recipes. I would also like to individually thank those loyal members, volunteers and supporters across the country who provided support in bringing the various elements of this book together: Joanne Brown; Heather-Ann Brown; Erik Buchanan; Bonnie Buxton; Elaine Comish; Maria Conforto; Pamela Douglas; Laura Eagle-LaDuke; Sylvia Fowles; Edith Freeman; Alice Gauvin; Patti Hanson; Laura Hennick; John Holland; Maura Keenan; Sally Ann Kerman; Lois Lavers; Sara Lawson; Emily Levitt; Meg Lloyd-Jones; Connie Luyt; Arlene Mahood; Elizabeth McKim; Ruth Miln; Victoria Mountain; Bob Olsen; Olga Peacock; Dr.

Allan Purdy; Jenny Reid; Dr. Gordon Robinson; Mary-Ann Roebellen; Andrea Rolston; Bill Ross; Nelly Sabbagh; Malcolm Sharp; Nelda Sharp; Dr. Ashfaq Shuaib; Donna-Lynn Turner; G. Joy Underwood; Grace Wood; and Dave Wright. I'd also like to recognize our dedicated volunteer Board of Directors: Georgina Kossivas, Dr. Marek Gawel, Karen Ormerod, Barbara Nawrocki, Dr. Rose Giammario, Dr. Gary Shapero and Debbie Drewett.

Special thanks should also go to Susan Folkins, my editor, for all her patience and advice. Thanks also to Anna Porter, Clare McKeon, Irene Worthington, Dr. Marek Gawel, Valerie South, Liba Berry and Cathy Fraccaro. All of your comments, suggestions and keen support were greatly appreciated.

I'd also like to recognize Astra Zeneca for their commitment to The Migraine Association of Canada and their assistance in making aspects of this project possible.

Many Toronto chefs also generously contributed recipes to our first cookbook, *Fabulous Cooking Ideas*. Some of their recipes are reprinted here. Thanks also to the chefs at North 44 for sharing their delicious recipe for Steamed Basmati Rice. I would also like to thank the authors of *HeartHealthy Cooking, Fare for Friends* and *Good Friends Cookbook* for granting us permission to reprint a few of their recipes.

Finally, I would like to thank our invaluable volunteers who provided us with their time, energy and support. We would not be able to continue to provide much needed information, education and services without you!

—Michele Sharp

More Than Just a Headache

Almost everyone has a headache now and then. The most common form of headache is tension type headache. Unlike migraine and other headache disorders, tension type headache is mild to moderate and is usually alleviated with rest and relaxation or over-the-counter pain relievers. Migraine, however, is a neurological disorder that involves a complex relationship between the blood supply to the brain and its nerve network.

Migraine occurs most often among people aged 20 to 50. The most common symptom associated with migraine is severe head pain made worse by routine activities, such as climbing stairs or bending over. The pain, often described by sufferers as "throbbing," is commonly felt on one side of the head, although it can switch sides during an attack or from one attack to the next. Many migraine sufferers feel nauseous and some vomit during an attack. Typically, sufferers are extremely sensitive to light, sound and odors, making ordinary events unbearable.

For the majority of migraine sufferers, or migraineurs, an untreated or unsuccessfully treated attack lasts 24 hours, although attacks can vary from two hours to several days. An average sufferer may have as many as 20 attacks every year; however, as many as 9 percent of sufferers experience 52 or more. During an attack and often leading up to and following an attack, migraineurs can become disabled, that is, it is necessary for them to completely or partially restrict their activities.

Migraine is more than a just a headache. In addition to waves of nausea and sensitivity to light, sound and odor, about one-fifth of migraine sufferers experience an "aura," a visual or sensory disturbance that acts as a warning sign to the oncoming headache. Other symptoms, often in the period of time leading up to the headache, include: irritability, depression, elation, excessive yawning, difficulty concentrating, dizziness, trouble with words, hyperactivity and food cravings (for more about the symptoms of migraine, see p. 17–18).

Why People Get Migraines

Experts have yet to pinpoint the exact cause of migraine, yet they do know it tends to run in families. In fact, over 50 percent of migraine sufferers have a close relative who experiences similar headaches, which indicates that migraine may be inherited. With the discovery of the gene responsible for familial hemiplegic migraine (a very rare form of the disorder), experts believe that with further research they may be able to generalize this information to the broader disorder. In the meantime, leading health experts describe individuals with migraine as wired differently, with a predisposition towards episodic migraine attacks. What triggers individual attacks varies between people and from one attack to the next.

What Happens in the Head

A complete understanding of the complex chain of physical events that precipitate a migraine attack is not fully understood. However, research in the past few decades has led to a better understanding of what happens in the head during a migraine attack. Researchers now know that certain chemicals in the brain—substance P, neurokinin A, and calcitonin gene-related peptide (CGRP), among others—are released and land on blood vessels. These chemicals cause the blood vessels to expand and send signals via the nerves to the brain, where the signals are processed to determine that the sensation is a painful one.

Types of Migraine

The two most common types of migraine are migraine without aura and migraine with aura. There are also several subtypes (atypical migraines) that are quite rare. They present themselves differently from the more common types, but researchers believe the triggers are the same.

Migraine without aura (previously called "common migraine")
Most migraineurs experience *migraine without aura*, usually described as throbbing head pain made worse by routine activities, such as climbing stairs or bending over; pain on one side of the head (although it can be on both sides or switch sides during an attack or from one attack to the next); nausea and/or vomiting; or extreme sensitivity to light, sound or smell. People afflicted with migraine frequently describe the pain as "hammering" or "pulsating."

More Than Just a Headache

Migraine with aura (previously called "classic migraine")

As many as 20 percent of migraine sufferers experience an aura before their migraine attack. As explained above, an aura is a visual or sensory disturbance that acts as a warning sign of the oncoming headache. Typical aura symptoms include: flashes of light, blurred vision, or blind spots spreading across the visual field. Some sufferers may feel tingling or numbness in the face, arms or hands. The symptoms usually fade within one hour as they give way to severe head pain. In some cases, however, a headache never follows. These migraine sufferers have migraine aura without headache.

Atypical migraine

There are also uncommon types of migraine such as familial hemiplegic migraine, basilar migraine and ophthalmoplegic migraine.

Familial hemiplegic migraine is the only type of migraine to have had a specific gene identified. This very rare atypical migraine is believed to result from a prolonged profound aura involving the brain. Symptoms often can mimic a stroke or tumor and range from a slight tingling or numbness on one side of the face or body to partial short-term paralysis. The headache is usually one-sided but the aftereffects of the aura can last for days. Rarely is it permanent.

Basilar migraine, also known as "basilar artery migraine," "Bickerstaff's migraine" and "syncopal migraine" is associated with several distinct aura symptoms. They include:

- Visual symptoms such as double vision
- Slurred speech
- Dizziness and/or vertigo
- Ringing in the ears
- Decreased hearing
- Numbness and tingling in limbs on both sides or severe weakness/paralysis of limbs on both sides
- Decreased level of awareness of surroundings

Ophthalmoplegic migraine is a very rare type of migraine. It involves repeated headaches with a paralysis of one or more cranial nerves that control pupil dilation and eye movement. People often experience double vision, and the symptoms may be mistaken for an aneurysm (a ballooning of the blood vessels in the head that can rupture and cause bleeding).

Other types of headache
Medication-induced headaches/rebound headaches

Medication-induced headaches or rebound headaches have become increasingly common. Migraine sufferers are often susceptible to developing these conditions. Scientists believe that when the level of analgesics (pain relievers) begins to lower in the body, the individual experiences a withdrawal reaction in the form of a headache. Increasing the level of analgesics relieves the headache, not because of the painkilling effect, but because it temporarily interrupts withdrawal. This condition can also occur with ergotamines. Only the complete elimination of analgesics or ergotamines in the system will end this vicious cycle. Discuss the options with your doctor.

Cluster headaches

Cluster headaches, another form of headache, should not be confused with migraine attacks. Unlike migraine, which occurs in nearly 17 percent of the North American population, cluster headache occurs in less than 1 percent of the population. Eighty-five percent of all cluster headache sufferers are men.

The symptoms of cluster headache are distinctly different from those of migraine. Attacks of cluster headache are grouped in a series of short, intensely severe bursts of pain, usually lasting 30 to 45 minutes and rarely lasting longer than four hours. Often occurring at night, the pain is sharp, piercing and debilitating. If you think you might be suffering from cluster headaches, consult your doctor and get a proper diagnosis. Cluster and migraine are distinct disorders with different symptoms and treatments.

Migraine in Women

Before puberty, the prevalence of migraine in both sexes is about equal. However, at the onset of puberty, the incidence of migraines in females increases dramatically. In adults, migraine is three times more prevalent in women than in men. It is believed that this is due to hormonal changes associated with the reproductive cycle.

For women whose migraines start at puberty, their migraines often show a lifelong connection to their menstrual cycle. Migraine attacks are linked to the menstrual cycle in about 60 percent of affected women (menstrually related migraine), and exclusive to the menstrual cycle in roughly 14 percent of affected women (true menstrual migraine). Both forms of menstrual migraine occur during or just after estrogen levels fall. Since estrogen levels fall after ovulation and before menstruation, this could account for headaches at these times. Depending on the woman's circumstances, doctors may prescribe hormone replacement therapy (HRT), which helps to stabilize estrogen levels during these critical times. In addition, some doctors prescribe non-steroidal anti-inflammatory drugs (NSAIDs), such as ibuprofen or naproxen, in the prevention of menstrual migraine.

For many women, their episodes of attacks improve with pregnancy or menopause. However, for some women migraine may appear for the first time during pregnancy. Often migraine will improve during the second and third trimesters, but throughout the pregnancy, and especially during the first trimester, medication must be approached cautiously and should be taken only on the advice of a doctor.

Oral contraceptives, which contain estrogen and progesterone, can induce, change or alleviate migraine. Their use can trigger the first migraine attack (most often in women with a family history of migraine) or exacerbate existing migraine, especially on those days when the woman is off the oral contraceptive.

During the early menopausal stage, tremendous fluctuations in estrogen can worsen migraine. Hormone replacement with estrogen, alone or in combination with progesterone, can either exacerbate migraine or relieve it. Cyclical hormone replacement therapy may trigger migraine in the days off the supplement, so continuous low doses of estrogen and progesterone are sometimes preferable. According to a recent North American study, about 62 percent of women experience fewer migraine headaches and a marked improvement after menopause; 28 percent felt no difference and 10 percent felt their migraines were worse.

Migraine in Children

If you're a parent, guardian or adult caring for a child with migraine, there may be some comfort in knowing that you're not alone. Approximately 4 to 5 percent of children suffer from migraine. While as many as one-third of children will outgrow migraine, many will go on to have migraine in adolescence. After age 12, the incidence of migraine increases in girls due to the role of hormones (see p. 13). By age 14, the rate for girls is approximately 15 percent, while the rate for boys hovers at 6 percent. Approximately 25 percent of adults with migraine report that their symptoms started before age 10.

Migraine in children is unique for several reasons. While identifying migraine in adults can be a challenge, diagnosing it in children is even more difficult. Children communicate their symptoms differently than adults. It's unlikely, for example, that you'll hear a child say, "I've been having a throbbing pain in my left temple accompanied by nausea two times a month." Instead, parents might notice that an otherwise playful child suddenly becomes introverted, irritable or covers his or her eyes.

Naturally, migraine affects children in different ways than adults. Children may miss school, stop participating in social activities, decline invitations to parties and, in some cases, may develop coping and communication problems. Adults caring for children with migraine can play a vital role in early detection, appropriate care, preventive measures and the development of a support network—all of which contribute to a positive attitude towards the disorder and enhance the sufferer's overall participation in life.

Sorting out the symptoms in children can be very difficult. As with adults, the most common form of migraine in children is *migraine without aura*, characterized by one or two-sided often frontal (across the forehead) moderate to severe head pain; sensitivity to light, sound and smells; and nausea or vomiting. Headaches in children are usually of shorter duration than those in adults. Your child's migraine may last for only one hour, and may be relieved after a long nap. In some cases, migraine can last for as long as two days.

The second most common form, *migraine with aura*, is characterized by visual or sensory disturbances. Blind spots, difficulty focusing and displays of flashing lights can be especially distressing for children. Other symptoms include numbness or tingling in the arms and hands or around the mouth. Some children will have the aura without the headache, with the possibility of developing the headache later in life.

Additional symptoms, possibly indicative of other types of migraine, such as double vision, eye pain, slurred speech, confusion, and weakness or paralysis, should be discussed with your doctor. Very young children may experience abdominal pain, intense vomiting, loss of balance or the feeling that everything around them is going very fast or very slow, or is unusually big or small. These symptoms may be the first expression of migraine, and can frighten or confuse both the child and adult.

Getting an accurate diagnosis and ruling out other causes is the first step in managing migraine (see p. 21). Many symptoms will disappear as the child matures and grows out of them, or as the more common features of migraine become more prominent. A visit to the doctor to review the child's history and symptoms will establish whether the child has migraine.

The next step is identifying triggers. No two children have exactly the same triggers, although there are a number of common ones. Susceptibility to triggers will change from time to time, depending on the child's overall emotional and physical well-being. For some children, diet is a key trigger; for others, stress, missed sleep or skipped meals, changes in weather, or changes to routine can bring on migraine. Reducing exposure to triggers is a key strategy for reducing the frequency of migraine.

During migraine attacks, children may find comfort in retreating to a darkened quiet room. Cold packs, fluids in moderation and a short nap may stave off an attack. When non-drug strategies are not successful, medication is an option when used as directed. In pediatric doses, over-the-counter medications such as ibuprofen (for older children or adolescents) or acetaminophen can help alleviate an attack. Acetylsalicylic acid (ASA) should not be used in children 12 years and under because of its association with Reye's syndrome (an often fatal disease of the brain that usually occurs in children following an acute viral infection).

Combination pain relievers containing codeine or migraine-specific medications (such as sumatriptan, zolmitriptan, naratriptan, rizatriptan or eletriptan) may be used in older children and adolescents when all other measures fail. Pain relievers should not be taken more than two days a week, in order to prevent rebound headaches (see p. 12). For chronic attacks or severe pain, emergency room treatment and/or preventive medications may be recommended.

In all cases, medication should be taken only at the advice of the child's physician. Some medications on the market have been tested only on adults and may not be suitable to children. Don't share your own or any one else's medication with your child.

It is important to develop, as much as possible, non-drug strategies to cope with migraine, such as rest, relaxation, regular routines and exercise. If tension or pressure at school or home is acting as a trigger, stress management, relaxation, biofeedback (see p. 23), hypnotherapy (see p. 23) or professional counseling can be effective. Developing early coping mechanisms will help your child deal effectively with migraine in the long run. As they say, an ounce of prevention is worth a pound of cure!

Diagnosis and Management of Migraine

Proper diagnosis of migraine is an important first step in taking control of your disorder. Many people (as many as 19 percent of sufferers) have never sought medical advice for their disorder and as many as 45 percent lapse from physician care.

The next step to managing this disorder is to learn as much as possible about it, about your triggers (whether they are dietary, hormonal or stress- or environment-related) and to take steps to change your lifestyle.

Diagnosing Migraine

First and foremost, managing migraine is about obtaining a diagnosis from a physician. According to a recent North American study, only 50 percent of migraine sufferers have actually been diagnosed and only 34 percent regularly consult a physician.

In 1988, the International Headache Society developed guidelines that considerably improved the diagnosis of migraine. Their diagnostic criteria for migraine included attacks lasting 4 to 72 hours, and some combination of the following symptoms:

- One-sided moderate to severe throbbing pain aggravated by movement;
- Nausea or vomiting;
- Sensitivity to light and sound; and
- Visual or sensory disturbances referred to as aura.

Other key headache syndromes were also identified, including rebound headache and cluster headache. See page 12 for more information on these types of headache.

Warning signs and symptoms
Many people actually experience symptoms and do not realize that they could be part of migraine. These should be checked by a physician. In

addition to the more easily recognized symptoms mentioned above, many people experience more subtle signs and symptoms with their attacks. These may be experienced prior to, as well as during, an attack and can include:

- Dizziness;
- General discomfort in the stomach and/or abdominal area;
- Depression, irritability, tension and/or other alteration in mood and outlook, sometimes with a feeling of detachment;
- Inability to concentrate;
- Sensitivity to light and sound;
- Feelings of extreme well-being with uncommon energy, vigor and a feeling of excitement preceding the attack;
- Excessive yawning;
- Unusual hunger, desire for snacks, especially sweets;
- Overtalkativeness or difficulty forming words, recalling words and incidents;
- Pain or numbness in neck and shoulder areas;
- Trembling;
- Patches or blotchy areas on skin, which looks like a rash;
- Unusual paleness or pallor (especially true with children); and
- Increase in weight, perhaps along with swelling in fingers and hands, waist, breasts, ankles or legs, or an increase in frequency and volume of urination.

These warning signs and symptoms are most frequently noted by physicians and those who suffer from migraine, and are sometimes called symptoms of the "prodrome" or aura. Individuals have suggested others that are peculiar to them. As with the more easily recognized symptoms of migraine, not everyone experiences all of these symptoms. When you discuss your migraine with your physician, it may help if you list the symptoms that refer specifically to you.

Triggers

A *trigger* is any internal or external influence that activates or aggravates a migraine attack. Most people find that a combination of triggers brings on an attack. Because people afflicted with migraine are sensitive to these influences, it is important to identify triggers and reduce or eliminate their impact as much as possible. It is also important to remember that triggers in and of themselves are not the cause of migraine and that migraine is a complicated biological disorder.

If you can readily identify your triggers, you will find it much easier to manage your migraine attacks. You can eliminate or avoid some triggers, reduce others, and brace for those over which you have no control. While some triggers, such as weather, are not controllable, they often work in combination with those that are controllable, such as food. For this reason, simply being aware of them will help you to manage your migraine.

Keeping a diary will help you to isolate your triggers. If you document your migraine attacks over a period of several months, you will probably notice that there is a pattern to your attacks. You should track the following items:

- Frequency of attacks
- Duration of attacks
- What the attacks felt like
- What made the pain worse and what made it better
- What other symptoms (nausea, vomiting, sensitivity to sound, light, etc.) you experienced
- What potential triggers (food, hormones, weather, stress, etc.) were you exposed to 24 to 48 hours in advance of an attack
- What medications or treatments you took and how they worked

Remember, though, that your triggers can change throughout life. Always be on the lookout for new ones and be open to the possibility that you may outgrow others.

The following list of triggers includes those that are most commonly known. Not all migraineurs will be affected by these triggers. Finding what is specific to you and avoiding or managing your triggers is the key. The five most common migraine triggers are:

Hormonal cycles or changes

- puberty
- menstruation
- birth control pills
- hormone replacement therapy
- peri-menopause

Changes in daily routine

- missing a meal
- sleeping more or less than usual

Stress

- experiencing an episode of emotional stress
- resting after an emotionally stressful period

Weather and environment

- changes in barometric pressure
- cigarette smoke (first and second-hand)

Dietary

- caffeine (coffee, tea, soft drinks) and, especially, caffeine withdrawal
- chocolate in any form
- fruits, especially citrus: oranges, lemons, limes, grapefruit, fermented dry fruits (raisins, figs, *etc.*), banana-peel extract, red plums, papaya and passion fruit
- beverages: beer, colored alcohol and wine (especially red, port, sherry, sweet white), dark rum, rye, brandy and scotch
- dairy products: cultured dairy products, such as sour cream and buttermilk; chocolate milk; acidophilus milk; aged cheese: Boursault, brick, Brie, Colby, Camembert, cheddar, Gouda, Gruyère, mozzarella, Parmesan, Emmentaler, Provolone, Romano, Roquefort and Stilton
- food additives: Aspartame—NutraSweet; MSG: Accent, ajinomoto, Chinese seasoning, flavorings (including natural), glutacyl, glutavene,

gourmet powder, hydrolyzed plant protein, hydrolyzed vegetable protein, kombo extract, mei-jing, RL-50, subu, vestin, wei-jing and Zest
- nuts: peanuts
- seeds: sesame, sunflower and pumpkin
- beans and vegetables: beans (lima, Italian, pole, broad, fava, navy, pinto, garbanzo, lentils, string), snow peas, chili peppers, pickles, olives, onions, garlic, peas and tomatoes
- miscellaneous: brewer's yeast
- meat, fish, poultry: Chicken and beef organ meats (liver and kidney), salted or dried fish (caplin, herring, cod), fermented sausage, bacon and processed meats (sodium nitrate)

Hint: Always read the labels of prepared foods, as many of these products contain additives such as MSG that may trigger a migraine attack. For a more detailed discussion of how to manage dietary triggers, see pp. 25–30.

Managing Migraine

After obtaining a diagnosis, you should take the following important steps in managing your migraine:

- identify your triggers by keeping a diary (see p. 31);
- keep a record of your triggers, as they can change over your life-time;
- optimize physical health by maintaining a healthy diet, exercising, keeping a regular sleep regime and taking medications correctly;
- optimize mental health and learn ways to manage the stress in your life;
- consult regularly with your physician regarding treatment options; and
- obtain up-to-date information from your physician or The Migraine Association of Canada.

Medication

When you discuss treatment options with your doctor, be aware that there are two basic types of migraine medication: symptomatic and preventive.

Symptomatic medications are taken to relieve the symptoms of an attack once it's in progress. These medications are usually more effective when they are taken in the early stages of the attack. The most common types of symptomatic medications that are available over the counter are acetylsalicylic acid (ASA), acetaminophen and ibuprofen.

Many symptomatic medications are currently available with a prescription, including a class of drugs called triptans. Triptan medications are known to the medical community as 5-HT (serotonin) receptor agonists. These medications work on the mechanism of migraine and relieve symptoms associated with migraine, such as headache pain, nausea/vomiting and sensitivity to light and sound. Triptan medications narrow (constrict) blood vessels in the head that expand (dilate) during a migraine attack. They are also thought to reduce the release of substances that cause blood vessels to become inflamed and to reduce transmission of pain impulses to the brain.

Preventive medications are taken daily to prevent or reduce the number of migraine attacks. Unlike symptomatic medications, they are not pain relievers. They work for many sufferers by correcting the underlying imbalances within the body believed to cause migraine. All preventive medications should be taken exactly as prescribed. They take time to start working, so before their effectiveness is evaluated, they should be given at least two months to start to work.

Preventive drugs include beta-blockers; calcium channel blockers; antidepressants; monoamine-oxidase inhibitors (MAOIs); antiserotonin agents; anti-inflammatory agents and anticonvulsants.

If you are interested in knowing more about these medications, consult your physician.

Complementary Therapies

A broad range of treatments for migraine do not fall within the category of conventional medicine. These include:

- biobehavioral treatment, such as biofeedback;
- relaxation therapy and cognitive-behavioral therapy;
- bodywork or manipulation, such as chiropractic, massage and acupuncture; and
- vitamin, mineral or herbal therapies, such as riboflavin, magnesium and feverfew.

These therapies are considered "complementary," or "non-pharmaco-logical," and for many play an important role in prevention and empow-erment of the sufferer. (Many migraineurs often feel powerless over their disorder and become frustrated or angry at the lack of validation from medical professionals, family members, employers or friends.) These approaches are particularly useful when conventional treatment is inade-quate, not tolerated or contraindicated. The appropriateness of using such therapies is based on availability and cost, and the motivation and commitment of the individual seeking treatment.

In seeking treatment, it is always important to get an initial diagnosis (see p. 17) and follow-up from a doctor. It is also important to return to a physician if there is a change in symptoms and before beginning new therapies. Beware of therapists who will not allow you to see anyone else at the same time or who have costly "miracle cures." Ask practitioners about their qualifications and whether their area of specialty is regulated by a professional organization. Ask them about the theory behind their method and talk to others who have undergone the same therapy.

Biofeedback allows you to learn to alter your physiological responses at will. Machines provide feedback about biological responses in the body, such as the contraction of scalp muscles and the circulation and tempera-ture of the hands or temple area. This information is then translated into a display—an audio tone or visual representation—that is "fed back" to the patient.

Relaxation therapy develops long-term skills for the prevention of migraine. Different methods include muscle relaxation, breathing exer-cises and directed imagery. Relaxation therapy is often combined with biofeedback.

Cognitive-behavioral therapy (CBT) helps migraine sufferers identify stressful circumstances and employ effective strategies for coping. Individuals identify and modify negative responses that may trigger or aggravate migraine. CBT may also help to limit the negative psychologi-cal consequences of chronic pain, such as depression and disability. Similarly, *hypnotherapy* reduces distressing sensory input, which can act as triggers or aggravators of migraine.

Chiropractic may relieve some migraine attacks. Too much or too little movement in the cervical or neck region can cause muscle spasms around the neck, which may lead to a migraine attack. Manipulation, exercise and physical therapy improve motion and can alleviate pain.

Massage has sedative and invigorating effects, increases range of motion, improves muscle tone and stimulates the release of endorphins, the body's natural painkillers. By massaging trigger points at the top of the neck and base of the skull, the tension associated with chronic pain may be relieved.

Acupuncture, a traditional Chinese medicine that uses needles to restore the balance of energy, is believed to block the transmission of pain and stimulate the release of endorphins.

Riboflavin* or Vitamin B[2] (400 mg) as well as *magnesium** (400–600 mg) may help to reduce the frequency and severity of migraine if taken on a daily basis.

Feverfew*, which comes from a plant belonging to the chrysanthemum family, may also help migraine sufferers. It is believed to work by reducing the release of a chemical closely linked to migraine; by inhibiting the secretion of prostaglandin, a substance involved in inflammation; and by stabilizing blood vessels, making them less sensitive to the release of chemicals. Brands of feverfew that bear Drug Identification Numbers (D.I.N.) are regulated for content and are considered more reliable sources for this product.

* Always check with your doctor if you are planning to use riboflavin, feverfew or magnesium.

Managing Dietary Triggers

While there is no known cure for migraines, understanding your triggers can help you take charge of your attacks so that you can get your life back. Not all people are affected by food triggers—but those who are affected will find that managing food triggers will ensure that you lead a life in which *you* are in control; identifying and avoiding your food triggers will help give you back a measure of control over your life.

Arguably, one of the most modifiable factors in migraine management is diet. While controversy remains around the relationship between the frequency and severity of migraines and the consumption of certain foods and substances, like additives and preservatives, contained in foods, there is little doubt that diet may play a significant role in triggering, or initiating, migraine. Adjusting your diet, *not* restricting your diet, will give you greater control over your attacks. Adjusting your diet, while ensuring that you are consuming an adequate amount of nutrients, will help you manage your migraine attacks, and stay healthy, whether you experience these headaches frequently or intermittently.

A substantial number of migraine sufferers experience an attack shortly after (or within 24 to 48 hours) consuming a particular food or combination of foods. As mentioned above, identifying your food triggers and then avoiding them in your diet is an important step in migraine management; in your taking back control. In this section, we will discuss food triggers, and how to identify them; migraines and MSG; and how to track your food triggers by keeping a trigger diary.

The information in the following pages should help you to recognize the foods, as well as the chemicals and additives contained in foods, that may trigger your migraines. Then turn to the recipe section for meal planning suggestions that will have you eating delicious foods that should not trigger an attack. You will soon recognize that you are not at the mercy of your migraines, and that you have, at your fingertips, and in your pantry, an arsenal with which to fight them.

It is important to note that the actual foods you eat are not necessarily the only triggers to your migraines; that is, they are usually collaborating with some of your other dietary habits, for example, skipping meals, fasting or delaying meals. Moreover, dietary triggers may also be interacting with other triggers, as discussed on page 20—environmental, stress, medication-related or hormonal.

Food Trigger or Food Allergy?

A food trigger is not a food allergy; a food allergy is an immune-system response to a protein contained in food. While some researchers believe that food allergies do cause headaches, most believe that they in themselves play no role in causing headache, but that the substances contained within some foods trigger the headache by changing the body's neurochemical balance, for example by altering the balance of the neurotransmitter (a kind of chemical messenger) serotonin, or by narrowing and then expanding blood vessels in the brain. It is important to note that since food allergies do not appear to cause migraines, allergy testing won't get you any further ahead in identifying your dietary triggers.

Anatomy of a Food Trigger

You eat a hot dog for lunch or go to your favorite Chinese restaurant for dinner, and within 24 hours, you suffer a debilitating migraine attack. Why does this happen? According to the *Canadian Medical Association Journal*, "[the] ingestion of foods containing nitrites, aspartame or monosodium glutamate, and the cumulative effect of eating foods with a high content of neurotransmitter precursors, such as tyramine, tyrosine and phenylalanine, are associated with the precipitation of migraine headache...." (CMAJ: 1997; 156(9)) Hot dogs, and other smoked or pre-served meats, like luncheon meats, ham, bacon and sausage, contain nitrites; and Chinese food is notorious for containing the flavor enhancer monosodium glutamate (see p. 29); both these substances are implicated in the triggering of migraine attacks. They cause neurological distur-bances that make the blood vessels in the brain swell, which further causes them to press on the surrounding nerves, which may trigger an attack.

Many foods that initiate migraine attacks contain substances, called vasoactive amines, that affect the body's blood vessels, especially those that supply blood to the brain. Vasoactive amines widen or narrow the blood vessels in the brain, which is responsible for the pain of the migraine headache. Food sources include any items that have been fer-mented; for example, ripened cheeses; these foods contain a substance known as tyramine. Tyramine can also be found in red organ meats (such as beef and chicken liver) and any pickled products.

Another amine implicated in the cause of migraines is phenyleth-lamine, a food source of which is chocolate in any form. Citrus fruits and their juices, also on the list of foods for some migraineurs to avoid, contain another headache-producing amine, synephrine.

Common sources of amine-containing foods include: fruits (avocado, banana, citrus fruits, pineapple, red-skinned fruits); vegetables (spinach, eggplant, skin of potatoes and tomatoes); beverages (dark alcoholic drinks, tea); dairy products (ripened cheeses, buttermilk, yogurt, sour cream); herbs and spices; and cured, pickled or marinated products. It is important to note that the amount of amine may be very slight and, in many cases, is not enough to trigger an attack.

The Migraineur's Pantry

A variety of foods and food additives are known to trigger migraine attacks (see pp. 20–21 for a list of the common dietary triggers), but it is important to note that not all these foods act as triggers to all migraineurs; people who are sensitive to one food may, in fact, be able to eat it in small quantities if they have managed to control other triggers. As mentioned earlier, food triggers often do not act alone, but in collaboration with other triggers (see p. 18).

Profiles of the usual suspects

Caffeine: Caffeine—or caffeine withdrawal—is often a trigger. In some cases, the ingestion of excessive amounts as part of a medication may be the culprit. Coffee and tea are common trigger foods, but remember that caffeine is also present in chocolate and soft drinks.

Chocolate: The more concentrated the chocolate is, the more likely it is to trigger a migraine. Unsweetened and bittersweet chocolate, for example, are the most concentrated. Some people can consume milk chocolate or white chocolate in modest amounts, and not risk suffering a migraine attack.

So, what's a chocoholic to do? Turn to the recipes section, and try

Carob Chip Cookies (p. 142) or No-Bake Carob-Oatmeal Macaroons (p. 143). These delectable "chocolate" treats will make even the most hardened chocoholic's mouth water.

Fruits: The most common triggers in this category are citrus fruits (lemons, limes, oranges and grapefruit). Some people can eat small quantities of these fruits and not suffer a migraine attack. Other food triggers in this category include: papaya, mangoes, kiwi, pineapple, plums, avocado and dried fruits that contain preservatives, for example, raisins, figs and dates. These foods also contain vasoactive amines, which, as mentioned earlier, affect the blood vessels that supply blood to the brain.

Try the Wild Cherry Tabbouleh (p. 107) or the Roasted Pears with Mint Anglaise (p. 124) for some fruity delights.

Alcohol: Alcoholic beverages can dilate blood vessels in the brain and for some trigger migraine attacks. Red wine and other "colored" alcoholic beverages, like dark rum, brandy, sherry, port and scotch, are more common culprits in triggering migraine attacks; the yeast contained in beer is also often implicated. Some migraineurs can tolerate white wine and other light-colored alcoholic drinks (vodka, for example), taken in modest amounts. It is important to remember that alcohol might negatively interact with medication you are taking for migraine as well as dehydrate you.

If you enjoy cooking with red wine, and need a substitute for this potential food trigger, use vodka or white wine instead; try the Phyllo-wrapped Chicken with Mushrooms and Spinach in Citron Vodka Sauce (p. 76), or the Scallops with White Wine and Tarragon Sauce (p. 95).

For a soothing, non-alcoholic drink, with medicinal qualities, try the Migraine Mellower (p. 148).

Dairy products: Cultured or fermented dairy products can be powerful triggers for some. Sources include yogurt and sour cream, chocolate milk, buttermilk, cultured butter, acidophilus milk and aged cheeses like Boursault, brick, Brie, Camembert, cheddar, Gouda, Gruyère, mozzarella, Parmesan, Emmentaler, Provolone, Romano, Roquefort and Stilton. If you want to use cheese in a recipe, try unaged or mild cheeses, like cottage cheese, goat cheese, farmer cheese and yogurt made from skim milk. Eggs are also a safe food choice, unlikely to trigger an attack. Also note that it is safe to drink 1% homogenized milk, 2% or skim.

If you find yourself yearning for cheese, try the delicious Warmed Goat Cheese Salad with Grilled Vegetables (p. 52), the Toasted Creamy Goat Cheese with Onion Confit (p. 54) or the marvelous Vegetable and Cheese Lasagna (p. 64).

Monosodium glutamate (MSG): This substance can be a powerful migraine trigger. Common sources include packaged foods, powdered or canned soups, bouillon cubes, frozen dinners and snack foods. There are also a number of hidden sources of MSG. Indeed, even if we carefully read food labels, and decide the ingredients are "safe," we are frequently unaware of the MSG that is hidden in some other substance that *is* listed. MSG often lurks in the guise of polysyllabic, indecipherable ingredients.

Here is a list of ingredients that always contain MSG:

Monosodium glutamate	Hydrolyzed protein
Sodium caseinate	Yeast extract
Yeast nutrient	Autolyzed yeast
Textured protein	Yeast food
Calcium caseinate	Hydrolyzed oat flour

Artificial sweeteners: These substances, especially aspartame (NutraSweet; Equal) have been found to trigger migraine attacks in some people. Aspartame is frequently used in diet soft drinks and in sugarless chewing gum. Other artificial sweeteners, such as cyclamate (Sugar Twin) and sucralose (Splenda) do not appear to trigger migraine attacks.

Nuts and seeds: If you are predisposed to migraines, peanuts (and peanut butter), and seeds, such as sesame, sunflower and pumpkin seeds, can be a trigger and may induce an attack. We include avocadoes in this category, although people usually think of them as a fruit.

Beans and vegetables: Onions and tomatoes (although these are considered by some to be a fruit) are often identified as migraine triggers. Other triggers in this category include: chili peppers, beans (lima, Italian, pole, broad, fava, navy, pinto, garbanzo, string), snow peas and lentils. Olives, pickles and sauerkraut have also been identified as possible culprits.

Delight in the fragrance and flavors of Steamed Basmati Rice with Crisp Potatoes, Sumac and Cumin (p. 106), Bulgur and Green Bean Salad with Herbed Vinaigrette (p. 108) or Charred Zucchini with Herbs, Garlic, and Ricotta (p. 103).

Breads and yeast-raised baked goods: These foods contain yeast, which may trigger a migraine attack. Commercially prepared breads appear to present less of a problem to migraineurs than their hot, fresh homemade counterparts. Before eating your beautiful homemade bread, let it sit for a while to cool; this may reduce its effect as a migraine trigger.

Try the Irish Scones (p. 117) or the Corn Bread (p. 119) for delicious breads that will not trigger a migraine attack.

Meat, poultry and fish: Fresh beef, poultry and fish are not implicated as migraine triggers, but organ meats, such as kidney and liver, may trigger an attack. Also in this category are processed or smoked meats, which contain nitrites, including hot dogs, luncheon meats, ham, bacon and sausage; and smoked, salted or pickled fish.

Sample the Curried Chicken with Peaches and Coconut (p. 69), the Roast Duck with Spiced Honey (p. 75) or the Yellowfin Tuna with Maple Mustard Sauce and Coriander Oil (p. 84) for some succulent entrees.

Miscellaneous: Although it seems rare, some people report suffering migraine attacks after consuming products containing food colorings and dyes, for example, as used in candies, powdered drinks, gelatin desserts; and after consuming vinegar, as contained in ketchup, mayonnaise and salad dressings.

Skipping Meals Can Trigger an Attack

If you are predisposed to migraines, don't skip meals, especially breakfast! A low blood sugar level caused by skipping meals, or other dietary practices, like irregular mealtimes or weight-loss diets, often trigger migraine attacks. Skipping breakfast is an especially dangerous practice if you're a migraineur; blood sugar levels are particularly low in the morning, and skipping breakfast can therefore trigger a headache later in the day. (Turn to the recipe section of the book and let yourself be tempted by the Big Loonie Pancakes, p. 121, or the Apple Pancakes, p. 122.)

To keep your blood sugar levels stable during the day, eat a number of small meals at regular intervals, rather than two or three large meals. Consume these meals no more than four or five hours apart. Refer to the recipe section of the book for snacks and meals that will keep your blood sugar levels from dipping too low, and thus avoid suffering a migraine attack. Sample the Yeast-Free Pretzels (p. 35) or the Herbed Pita Chips (p. 36) for a migraine-free dietary pick-me-up.

Tracking the Culprits: Your Food Trigger Diary

Once you've examined the contents of your pantry and refrigerator, and thought carefully about your food consumption patterns and all your triggers, you're well on the way to identifying the foods and beverages that may be responsible for triggering your migraine attacks. A diary in which you diligently track all the foods you eat each day will help you further identify the items to steer clear of if you want to avoid an attack.

Keeping a diary will help you determine your "trigger threshold"—the number of triggers you can be exposed to before experiencing an attack. For example, you may drink a cup of coffee and not end up in the grips of a migraine; but you may find that drinking a second cup, skipping a meal and being overtired or overstressed will push you over the threshold, and you will experience a migraine attack.

In your diary, record:

- the food (or beverage) you consumed (include alcoholic beverages and those containing caffeine);
- the amount you consumed; and
- the time you consumed it. (Note that it may take your body 24 to 48 hours to react to a trigger.)

Also record any headaches you experience, and note:

- date;
- time of day;
- location of head pain (behind the eyes; squeezing head like a band; pounding on either side of head; at top of head, radiating down sides);
- duration;
- frequency;
- severity; and
- other symptoms (vomiting, nausea, sensitivity to light and sound).

You should also document other triggers such as weather, stress, hormonal fluctuations and so on, since, as mentioned earlier, food triggers often work with other trigger accomplices.

Testing your triggers

As a pattern emerges, you may notice a correlation between your consumption of a food or beverage and the incidence and severity of your migraine attacks. Add these to your food triggers list and avoid eating them; find delicious substitutes in the recipe section of this book.

Avoid in your diet the triggers identified in your diary, then re-introduce each of your "forbidden" foods. If you find you experience no symptoms when the food is not included in your diet, and the symptoms reappear when the food is re-introduced, this food may be one of those triggering your migraine attack.

Documenting the foods and beverages you consume is not a complicated task, and is well worth the effort in helping you get your life back.

To obtain a copy of a migraine diary, contact an association near you (see pp. 154–157 for a complete List of Resources).

Managing Dietary Triggers

Checklist for avoiding migraines

1. *Know* your food triggers: keep a list of them at hand, perhaps on the refrigerator door, where you can see them each time you're tempted to reach for that chocolate ice cream or a hunk of cheddar.

2. *Document* the foods you eat each day, in a migraine diary, in order to identify the substances that may be initiating your migraine attacks.

3. *Note* all your triggers, including your sleep patterns, changes in weather, hormonal fluctuations, and the incidence of stressful events.

4. *Read* food labels when you're food shopping, to make sure trigger ingredients are not contained in the food item you are about to purchase. And be aware of hidden food triggers.

5. *Enjoy* the delectable, mouthwatering, migraine-free recipes in this book.

The Last Word. . . .

It is a challenge living comfortably with migraine; in fact, the idea that one can live comfortably with these often debilitating headaches may appear to be absurd, an impossibility. However, by controlling the modifiable factors in your daily life, by managing your triggers and discussing treatment options with your doctor, you can regain control of your life.

You may wonder how on earth you're going to find anything to eat or how you're ever going to plan a meal, since everything you enjoy seems to be a potential trigger. The answer is in some of the suggestions made in this section and in the recipe portion of this cookbook. Use the recipes in the following pages to prepare mouthwatering dishes that are free of widely acknowledged food triggers. You will find recipes for appetizers and snacks, soups and salads, meatless main courses, meat and poultry, fish and seafood, vegetables and side dishes, breads, desserts and baked goods, and beverages. Plan your meals using these recipes, and you will enjoy eating wonderful foods with the knowledge that you are not setting yourself up for a migraine attack.

How to Use This Cookbook

The recipes found within these pages are delicious and nutritious and range from the easy-to-create to the more sophisticated.

Wherever possible, we have attempted to minimize the number of potential food triggers contained in the recipes or we have suggested substitutions. To help you readily identify the recipes that are appropriate for you, we have included a trigger coding system for each recipe. It outlines the ten most common triggers and indicates the specific triggers that have been avoided or eliminated. For example, if a recipe contains no citrus fruit (lemon, lime, orange or grapefruit), it is checked as being citrus-free.

Each recipe also contains a nutritional analysis and all recipes are calculated per serving size, unless otherwise indicated. Where there is a choice, the nutritional analysis is based on a smaller quantity and on the first ingredient. When ingredients are optional, they are not included in the analysis. Milk is calculated at 2% unless otherwise indicated.

Bon appétit!

Appetizers and Snacks

Yeast-Free Pretzels

A wonderful alternative to bread pretzels for anyone who finds that yeast is a trigger.

2	eggs, separated	2
¼ cup	softened margarine	50 mL
2 cups	all purpose flour	500 mL
	Salt and pepper	
	Milk	
	Coarse salt	

In small bowl, beat egg whites until stiff, but not dry. In separate bowl, beat egg yolks until lemony.

In large bowl, with your hands or spoon, work egg yolks and margarine into flour to form dough-like mixture. Fold in egg whites. Season with salt and pepper to taste. Roll out dough, then slice and shape into pretzels on greased baking sheet. Brush with milk and sprinkle with salt. Bake in 350°F (180°C) oven for about 10 minutes, turning over once. Serve the pretzels warm.

Makes about six 6-inch (15 cm) pretzels.

This recipe is FREE of the following triggers (marked ✔)

Caffeine ✔
Chocolate ✔
Citrus fruits ✔
Red wine ✔
Aged cheese ✔
MSG & Nitrates ✔
Aspartame ✔
Nuts ✔
Onions & Garlic ✔
Yeast ✔

Nutrients per serving (1 pretzel):
Calories: 236
Protein: 7 grams
Fat: 8 grams
Carbohydrate: 34 grams

Herbed Pita Chips

These crispy and flavorful chips are ideal for a light snack.

8	large pita pockets	8
1 cup	melted butter	250 mL
1 tsp	each dried oregano, marjoram, basil, and parsley flakes	5 mL

Separate each pita pocket into two thin rounds. With scissors, cut rounds into eighths. In small bowl, combine melted butter, oregano, marjoram, basil, and parsley; brush on pita pieces. Place on greased baking sheet and bake in 300°F (150°C) oven for 30 minutes.

Makes about 128 pita chips.

Nutrients per serving (1 pita chip):
Calories: 30
Protein: trace
Fat: 2 grams
Carbohydrate: 3 grams

Vegetable Platter with Olive Oil Dip (*Pinzimonio*)

An Italian idea, this healthy, easy-to-prepare appetizer consists simply of an assortment of fresh vegetables and extra virgin olive oil.

Fresh vegetables, such as carrots, cucumbers,
   red or yellow peppers, cherry tomatoes, fennel bulbs,
   and radishes, washed and cut up
Extra virgin olive oil
Salt
Crusty bread (optional)
Prosciutto, sliced paper thin (optional)

This recipe is FREE of the following triggers (marked ✔)
Caffeine ✔
Chocolate ✔
Citrus fruits ✔
Red wine ✔
Aged cheese ✔
MSG & Nitrates
Aspartame ✔
Nuts ✔
Onions & Garlic ✔
Yeast

Arrange vegetables on platter. (The quantity is flexible, depending on how many people you are serving.) Drizzle olive oil onto individual plates and season to taste with salt. The vegetables can then be dipped into the olive oil. For additional flavor, serve with bread and prosciutto, although you'll want to avoid the latter if nitrates are a trigger for you.

VARIATION: **Many vegetables can be served raw, but you may want to blanch some vegetables, such as green beans, sugar peas, or broccoli florets.**

Hummus

Nutrients per serving (1 tbsp/15 mL serving):
Calories: 59
Protein: 2 grams
Fat: 3 grams
Carbohydrate: 6 grams

A Middle Eastern specialty, hummus is ideal served with Herbed Pita Chips (see p. 36) or as a vegetable dip.

1	14-oz (398 mL) can chick peas	1
⅓ cup	(approx.) hot water	75 mL
1	large lemon, juiced	1
2	cloves garlic	2
¼ cup	tahini	50 mL
	Virgin olive oil	
	Salt	
	Chili powder	

Drain and thoroughly rinse chick peas. Process in food processor, gradually adding hot water to make light consistency.

Add lemon juice, garlic, tahini, about 1 tablespoon (15 mL) of oil; season with salt to taste. Process until well blended and smooth. Taste and adjust seasonings, if necessary.

Transfer spread to serving bowl and garnish with chili powder.

Makes about 1 cup (250 mL).

VARIATION: **Fresh chopped parsley and lightly toasted pine nuts can also be used as garnishes.**

Shiitake Perogies with Sweet Ginger Sauce

These dainty, vegetarian perogies make an elegant and tasty appetizer. If MSG is a trigger, make sure you use a naturally brewed soy sauce or Homemade Soy Sauce (see p. 114).

1 cup	mashed potatoes (cold leftovers are perfect)	250 mL
1 cup	shiitake mushrooms, finely chopped (stems removed)	250 mL
1	clove garlic, minced	1
½ tsp	fresh coriander leaves, finely chopped	2 mL
1	pkg oriental dumpling wrappers (available at oriental food stores; they're round and white)	1

Sweet Ginger Sauce

2 tsp	soy sauce (naturally brewed or Homemade, p. 114)	10 mL
1 tsp	cornstarch	5 mL
½ cup	chicken or vegetable stock (see pp. 110–111)	125 mL
1 tsp	minced ginger	5 mL
2 tsp	granulated sugar	10 mL
1 tsp	butter	5 mL

This recipe is FREE of the following triggers (marked ✔)

Caffeine ✔
Chocolate ✔
Citrus fruits ✔
Red wine ✔
Aged cheese ✔
MSG & Nitrates ✔
Aspartame ✔
Nuts ✔
Onions & Garlic
Yeast ✔

Nutrients per serving:
Calories: 53
Protein: 1 gram
Fat: 1 gram
Carbohydrate: 10 grams

In large bowl, mix mashed potatoes with mushrooms, garlic, and coriander. Place 1 tablespoon (15 mL) of this mixture on each dumpling wrapper and wet rim with water. Close and press together to seal; boil or shallow fry dumplings on high heat for about 3 minutes or until cooked through. Set aside.

Sweet Ginger Sauce: Combine soy sauce and cornstarch. Add to remaining ingredients in saucepan. Bring sauce to boil; simmer until thickened.

Serve Shiitake Perogies in pool of sauce, with sauce poured over them, or tossed with sauce.

Makes 6 servings.

MAKE AHEAD: Shiitake Perogies can be prepared up to a day ahead and stored in an airtight container in the refrigerator. Cook perogies just prior to serving. The sauce can also be prepared a day or two in advance, stored in the refrigerator, and heated prior to serving.

Shrimp Rissoles

Nutrients per serving :
Calories: 742
Protein: 18 grams
Fat: 38 grams
Carbohydrate: 82 grams

Delicate morsels of shrimp inside a lightly fried golden crust—these scrumptious appetizers will keep your guests coming back for more. If lemon juice is a trigger for you, you might consider using finely chopped lemon grass instead.

Filling

2 tbsp	olive oil	25 mL
1	onion, chopped	1
2	cloves garlic, chopped	2
1 cup	baby shrimp, cleaned	250 mL
1 cup	water	250 mL
4	eggs	4
1 cup	milk	250 mL
2 tbsp	cake flour	25 mL
2 tbsp	cornstarch	25 mL
	Salt and pepper	
	Lemon juice, to taste	
2 tbsp	chopped parsley	25 mL
Pinch	nutmeg	Pinch

Dough

2 cups	water	500 mL
2 cups	milk	500 mL
⅔ cup	vegetable shortening	150 mL
¼ cup	butter	50 mL
Pinch	salt	Pinch
	Pepper	
2-⅔ cups	all-purpose flour	650 mL
⅔ cup	cake flour	150 mL
⅔ cup	cornstarch	150 mL
¼ cup	fine breadcrumbs	50 mL

FILLING:

In medium saucepan, heat olive oil over medium heat. Add onion and garlic; cook until onions are golden. Add shrimp and cook for 1 minute. Add water, stirring until mixture comes to a boil.

Meanwhile, in bowl, mix together 2 eggs, milk, cake flour, and cornstarch. Add to mixture in saucepan.

Add salt and pepper to taste, lemon juice, parsley, and nutmeg and bring to boil. Remove from heat and let mixture cool.

DOUGH:

In large pot, combine water, milk, shortening, butter, salt, and pepper to taste. Bring mixture to boil. Add all-purpose flour, cake flour, and cornstarch; mix gradually until pasty. Remove from heat.

With rolling pin on floured surface, roll out dough until ⅛ inch (3 mm) thick all across. Cut into 3-inch (8 cm) circles using round cookie cutter. Place spoonful (15 mL) of filling in center of each circle; fold over to form half-moon shape and seal dough.

Brush stuffed pastry with two remaining beaten eggs and toss rissoles in breadcrumbs.

Deep fry rissoles (oil must be at least 325°F/160°C) until golden. Let cool and serve on platter lined with lettuce leaves.

Makes 6 servings.

MAKE AHEAD: **The shrimp filling can be prepared up to 2 days ahead and stored in the refrigerator. The rissoles can be assembled a day ahead, refrigerated, and cooked just before serving.**

Grilled Gravlax
with Mustard Dill Sauce

Nutrients per serving
(1 pretzel):
Calories: 416
Protein: 21 grams
Fat: 36 grams
Carbohydrates: 2 grams

The sweetly pungent dill sauce goes well with gravlax. Some mustards contain MSG, so watch for this potential trigger—the same amount of dry mustard can often be used instead.

1 lb	gravlax, cut into 8 slices	500 g
	Extra virgin olive oil	

Mustard Dill Sauce

1 tsp	dry mustard powder	5 mL
2 tbsp	water	25 mL
2 tbsp	grainy Dijon mustard	25 mL
1	egg yolk	1
1 tsp	granulated sugar	5 mL
½ cup	vegetable oil	125 mL
2 tbsp	chopped fresh dill	25 mL
	Dill sprigs	

Mustard Dill Sauce: In small bowl, dissolve dry mustard powder in water. Add Dijon mustard, egg yolk, and sugar. Gradually whisk in oil; add dill.

Lightly oil gravlax; place on preheated grill. Grill for 1 to 2 minutes per side or until lightly seared.

Place 2 slices of gravlax on individual salad plates; spoon some mustard sauce around gravlax. Garnish with sprig of fresh dill.

Makes 4 servings.

Soups and Salads

Cream of Mushroom Soup

An earthy and satisfying beginning to a fall or winter meal. The recipe calls for a small amount of onion, but this ingredient can be omitted if it is a trigger for you.

2 tbsp	butter	25 mL
1 tsp	chopped onion	5 mL
1 cup	chopped mushrooms	250 mL
3 tbsp	all-purpose flour	50 mL
1 tsp	salt	5 mL
Pinch	pepper	Pinch
2 cups	chicken stock (see p. 111)	500 mL
2 cups	milk	500 mL

This recipe is FREE of the following triggers (marked ✔)

Caffeine ✔
Chocolate ✔
Citrus fruits ✔
Red wine ✔
Aged cheese ✔
MSG & Nitrates ✔
Aspartame ✔
Nuts ✔
Onions & Garlic
Yeast ✔

In saucepan, melt butter over medium heat; sauté onion and mushrooms. Blend in flour and add salt and pepper. Stir in chicken stock and milk. Heat until steaming and serve immediately.

Makes 4 servings.

Nutrients per serving:
Calories: 148
Protein: 6 grams
Fat: 8 grams
Carbohydrate: 13 grams

Cream of Spinach Soup

Nutrients per serving:
Calories: 112
Protein: 4 grams
Fat: 8 grams
Carbohydrate: 6 grams

This soup is rich but light and tastes as fresh as spinach itself.

4 cups	chicken stock (see p. 111)	1 L
2 to 3 cups	fresh spinach, chopped	500 to 750 mL
1	slice onion (omit if onion is trigger)	1
1 cup	(approx.) 10% cream	250 mL
	Salt and pepper	
	Fresh parsley for garnish	

In large saucepan, simmer chicken stock, spinach, and onion for about 10 minutes.

In blender, process stock mixture until smooth. Return mixture to saucepan and heat. Add cream until soup is of desired consistency. Add salt and pepper to taste. Serve, garnished with chopped parsley.

Makes 4 servings.

Pumpkin Bisque

This smooth, full-flavored soup is a perfect make-ahead first course for an autumn dinner party. It also freezes well and can be reheated in the microwave.

2 tbsp	butter	25 mL
2	leeks (white part) thinly sliced	2
½ cup	each diced carrot and parsnip	125 mL
5 cups	chicken stock (see p. 111)	1.25 L
2-½ cups	pumpkin puree	625 mL
1 tsp	dried thyme	5 mL
½ tsp	salt	2 mL
¼ tsp	pepper	1 mL
Pinch	hot pepper flakes (if desired)	Pinch
½ cup	milk	125 mL
2 tbsp	snipped chives	25 mL

This recipe is FREE of the following triggers (marked ✔)

Trigger
Caffeine ✔
Chocolate ✔
Citrus fruits ✔
Red wine ✔
Aged cheese ✔
MSG & Nitrates ✔
Aspartame ✔
Nuts ✔
Onions & Garlic
Yeast ✔

Nutrients per serving:
Calories: 108
Protein: 3 grams
Fat: 4 grams
Carbohydrate: 15 grams

In large saucepan, melt butter over low heat. Add leeks, carrots, and parsnips, and cook until softened, about 10 minutes.

Stir in stock, pumpkin puree, thyme, salt, pepper, and hot pepper flakes, if using.

Bring to boil, reduce heat, cover, and simmer for 10 minutes or until vegetables are very soft.

In blender or food processor, puree in batches until smooth. Return to saucepan. Stir in milk; heat gently until hot (do not boil). Taste and adjust seasoning. Serve, sprinkled with chives.

Makes 8 servings.

Vichyssoise

This recipe is FREE of the following triggers (marked ✔)

Caffeine ✔	
Chocolate ✔	
Citrus fruits ✔	
Red wine ✔	
Aged cheese ✔	
MSG & Nitrates ✔	
Aspartame ✔	
Nuts ✔	
Onions & Garlic	
Yeast ✔	

Nutrients per serving:
Calories: 259
Protein: 6 grams
Fat: 7 grams
Carbohydrate: 43 grams

This potato and leek soup is best served very cold. The potatoes provide a rich thickness and the leeks a delicate flavor. If onions are a trigger, you might want to skip this recipe because leeks and chives are in the same family of vegetables.

1 tbsp	butter	15 mL
4	leeks, finely sliced	4
1	large onion, finely sliced	1
4	medium potatoes, peeled and diced	4
2 cups	chicken stock (see p. 111)	500 mL
	Salt and pepper	
½ cup	cream	125 mL
	Chives or parsley	

In saucepan, melt butter over medium heat; cook leeks and onions until transparent (do not brown). Add diced potatoes and chicken stock. Season with salt and pepper to taste and cook slowly, for about 30 minutes or until potatoes are tender.

In blender or food processor, puree until smooth.

Refrigerate, covered, until cold, at least 2 hours. Stir in cream.

Adjust seasoning, if necessary, and ladle soup into chilled bowls. Sprinkle with chives or chopped parsley before serving.

Makes 4 servings.

Curried Winter Vegetable Soup

This hearty soup can be adapted to meet specific dietary needs. For a little variety, add some chopped kale or leftover lettuce and serve with toasted French bread. It's great served with warm biscuits (see Healthy Biscuits on p. 116).

1-½ tbsp	butter	20 mL
1 tsp	each cumin, curry, rosemary, pepper, and sage	5 mL
4 to 6	cloves garlic, minced	4 to 6
1	large leek, chopped	1
4 cups	chicken or vegetable stock (see pp. 110 and 111)	1 L
1 cup	water	250 mL
1	medium rutabaga, peeled and cubed	1
1 cup	split lentils (red and/or yellow)	250 mL
2	medium sweet potatoes, peeled and diced	2
1	medium waxy potato, peeled and diced	1
2	medium carrots, peeled and sliced	2
1	medium parsnip, peeled and sliced	1
¼ cup	coconut milk (or regular milk if desired)	50 mL
2 tbsp	finely chopped cilantro or parsley	25 mL

This recipe is FREE of the following triggers (marked ✔)

Caffeine ✔
Chocolate ✔
Citrus fruits ✔
Red wine ✔
Aged cheese ✔
MSG & Nitrates ✔
Aspartame ✔
Nuts ✔
Onions & Garlic ✔
Yeast ✔

Nutrients per serving:
Calories
Protein g
Fat g
Carbohydrates g

In large stockpot, melt butter. Stir in cumin, curry, rosemary, pepper, and sage. Add garlic and leek. Cook over low heat, 2 to 5 minutes or until leek is tender. Add stock, water, rutabaga, and lentils. Bring to boil, slowly; reduce heat to simmer for 10 minutes, covered. Add potatoes, carrots, and parsnip.

Simmer, covered, for 25 to 40 minutes or until potatoes, carrots, and parsnips are tender. Remove from heat; allow to cool slightly until all bubbling has stopped. Mash with potato masher until consistency is partly chunky. Stir in coconut milk or milk (if using) and cilantro or parsley. Return to heat briefly to re-warm and serve.

Makes 6 to 8 servings.

VARIATIONS: These are endless as any vegetable can easily be added or substituted in this recipe. Cooked meat can also be added. Barley can be used instead of the lentils, but more cooking time should be allowed.

Easy Fish Chowder

Nutrients per serving:
Calories: 392
Protein: 23 grams
Fat: 16 grams
Carbohydrate: 39 grams

Serve this nutritious chowder with crackers or crusty bread.

2 tbsp	butter	25 mL
4	medium potatoes, diced	4
1 cup	thinly sliced celery	250 mL
1 cup	grated carrot	250 mL
1 tsp	rosemary	5 mL
	Salt and pepper	
½ lb	fish fillets (cod, haddock, or any firm white fish), or 1 can (5 oz/142 g) baby clams (with juice)	250 g
2 cups	whole evaporated milk	500 mL

In large saucepan, melt butter over medium heat. Lightly sauté potatoes, celery, and carrot. Cover with water (or clam juice, if using); add rosemary and salt and pepper to taste. Simmer until tender.

Add fish, cut into pieces, and simmer until fish flakes easily when tested with fork. Stir in milk and heat through without boiling. Just before serving, add salt and pepper to taste.

Makes about 4 servings.

Roasted Potato Salad

A fresh and satisfying alternative to your mom's potato salad. Serve with a loaf of fresh, crusty bread.

1	whole garlic head	1
1 tbsp	(approx.) olive oil	15 mL
	Salt and pepper	
2 lb	potatoes, scrubbed and cut into chunks	1 kg
1	red pepper	1
⅓ cup	(approx.) chopped red onion	75 mL

Balsamic Vinaigrette

¼ cup	olive oil (or canola oil)	50 mL
2 tbsp	balsamic vinegar (or cider vinegar— if using cider, add 2 tbsp/25 mL brown sugar)	25 mL
1 tsp	Dijon mustard (or the same amount of dry mustard, if MSG is a trigger)	5 mL
1 tsp	fresh thyme	5 mL
Pinch	each cayenne, salt, and pepper	Pinch

This recipe is FREE of the following triggers (marked ✔)

Caffeine ✔
Chocolate ✔
Citrus fruits ✔
Red wine ✔
Aged cheese ✔
MSG & Nitrates
Aspartame ✔
Nuts ✔
Onions & Garlic
Yeast ✔

Nutrients per serving
(when recipe serves 6):
Calories: 234
Protein: 4 grams
Fat: 10 grams
Carbohydrate: 32 grams

Cut half inch (1 cm) off garlic head and place garlic in small baking dish. Drizzle with some oil and season with salt and pepper. Cover with aluminum foil. Bake in 300°F (150°C) oven for 1-½ hours, or until tender when squeezed. Let cool.

In roasting pan in 425°F (220°C) oven, heat 1 tbsp (15 mL) oil until hot. Add potatoes; toss to coat. Roast for 35 minutes or until soft and golden, turning often.

Vinaigrette: In small bowl, whisk together ingredients.

Squeeze roasted garlic pulp into serving bowl. Add potatoes, red pepper, onion, and vinaigrette. Toss. Adjust seasoning. Serve warm or at room temperature.

Makes 4 to 6 servings.

Grated Root Vegetable Salad with Roasted Apple Dressing

This recipe is FREE of the following triggers (marked ✔)
Caffeine ✔
Chocolate ✔
Citrus fruits ✔
Red wine ✔
Aged cheese ✔
MSG & Nitrates ✔
Aspartame ✔
Nuts ✔
Onions & Garlic ✔
Yeast ✔

Nutrients per serving:
Calories: 174
Protein: 2 grams
Fat: 6 grams
Carbohydrate: 28 grams

The unusual dressing gives this salad an exceptional flavor.

2	Granny Smith apples, peeled and cored	2
	Olive oil, as needed	
	Sea salt	
2	medium red beets, peeled	2
2	parsnips, peeled	2
1	carrot, peeled	1
1	celeriac, peeled	1
1	head butter lettuce, or other preferred soft lettuce	1

DRESSING:

Peel and core apples and arrange neatly in lightly oiled skillet.

Season with sea salt, if desired, and cook over medium-high heat, turning occasionally, until tender and golden (do not allow to burn).

Transfer cooked apples to food processor. Process at high speed. Gradually pour in olive oil, incorporating until dressing is creamy.

SALAD:

Grate vegetables, keeping each vegetable separate and covered until ready for plating.

Spread some apple dressing on individual salad plates and arrange small mounds of grated vegetables around rim. Place lettuce leaves in center of plate; drizzle with some of remaining dressing.

Makes 4 servings.

MAKE AHEAD: **The apple dressing can be prepared earlier in the day and refrigerated.**

KITCHEN POINTER: **Remember to shred the vegetables as thinly as possible using a mandoline with the julienne attachment, or other favorite vegetable grater.**

Middle Eastern Salad

This is a fantastic salad with refreshingly different tastes.

½	cucumber, chopped	½
	Salt and pepper	
¼ cup	extra virgin olive oil	50 mL
1 tbsp	lemon juice	15 mL
1	clove garlic, minced	1
1	tomato, finely chopped	1
½	red pepper, chopped	½
¼ cup	thinly sliced scallion	50 mL
2 tbsp	finely chopped fresh parsley	25 mL
3 tbsp	finely chopped fresh mint	50 mL

This recipe is FREE of the following triggers (marked ✔)

Caffeine	✔
Chocolate	✔
Citrus fruits	
Red wine	✔
Aged cheese	✔
MSG & Nitrates	✔
Aspartame	✔
Nuts	✔
Onions & Garlic	
Yeast	✔

In sieve, sprinkle cucumber with pinch of salt. Let drain for 20 minutes, and pat dry.

In large bowl, whisk together olive oil, lemon juice, garlic, and salt and pepper to taste. Stir in tomato, red pepper, scallion, parsley, and mint. Add cucumber. Toss to combine well. Garnish with mint sprigs and serve with toasted pita or falafel.

Makes 2 servings.

Nutrients per serving:
Calories: 251
Protein: 2 grams
Fat: 23 grams
Carbohydrate: 9 grams

Warmed Goat Cheese Salad with Grilled Vegetables

This recipe is FREE of the following triggers (marked ✔)
Caffeine ✔
Chocolate ✔
Citrus fruits ✔
Red wine ✔
Aged cheese ✔
MSG & Nitrates
Aspartame ✔
Nuts ✔
Onions & Garlic ✔
Yeast

Nutrients per serving:
Calories: 184
Protein: 10 grams
Fat: 8 grams
Carbohydrate: 18 grams

This fanciful salad brings together a wonderful assortment of vegetables. The same amount of dry mustard can be used instead of Dijon mustard, if MSG is a trigger.

1	small green zucchini	1
2	small eggplant	2
1	small red or green pepper, seeds removed	1
1	small fennel bulb, top stems removed	1
4 oz	tube Woolwich goat cheese	113 g
1	egg	1
2 tbsp	water	25 mL
½ cup	Italian-style breadcrumbs	125 mL
1 cup	baby organic mixed salad greens	250 mL

Optional Salad Dressing

½ cup	raspberry vinegar	125 mL
1 tbsp	Dijon mustard	15 mL
1 tbsp	Italian-style herbs (basil, thyme, oregano, *etc.*)	15 mL
¾ cup	extra virgin olive oil	175 mL
	Salt and pepper	

Trim ends off both zucchini and eggplant. Cut zucchini and eggplant diagonally lengthwise into even-sized pieces.

Cut pepper lengthwise into 1 inch (2.5 cm) wide strips.

Cut fennel bulb into quarters, then cut each quarter in half. Blanch fennel pieces in boiling salted water for approximately 5 minutes. Set aside.

Remove goat cheese from protective wrapper. Cut into even-sized pieces (see Pointer below).

Break egg into bowl; add approximately 2 tbsp (25 mL) water and whisk together to create egg wash.

Dip pieces of goat cheese into egg wash; thoroughly cover with bread-crumbs and set aside.

Salad Dressing (optional): In bowl, mix vinegar, Dijon, and herbs; whisk vigorously while slowly adding oil. Season with salt and pepper to taste.

To assemble salad: Toss vegetables with a little oil and season with salt and pepper. Grill vegetables over high heat or under broiler, turning them over when they are slightly charred, after approximately 2 minutes.

Meanwhile, pour desired amount of dressing over salad greens and toss to thoroughly coat.

Place equal amounts of salad onto individual salad plates and arrange vegetables around salad. Warm goat cheese under broiler for approximately 1 minute; place on top of salad.

Makes 2 to 4 servings.

MAKE AHEAD: **The dressing can be made earlier in the day. It will keep for 1 week if stored in an airtight container in the refrigerator.**

KITCHEN POINTER: **Goat cheese is best cut with dental floss to avoid breakage.**

Toasted Creamy Goat Cheese with Onion Confit

Toasted on eggplant with onion confit, the creamy goat cheese has a marvelous flavor.

Nutrients per serving:
Calories: 441
Protein: 12 grams
Fat: 41 grams
Carbohydrate: 6 grams

½ cup	olive oil	125 mL
2	onions, finely sliced	2
3	cloves garlic, finely chopped	3
1	bay leaf	1
¼ cup	dry white wine (optional)	50 mL
2 tbsp	white wine vinegar	25 mL
	Salt and pepper	
¼ cup	vegetable oil	50 mL
1 tbsp	balsamic vinegar	15 mL
2	sprigs fresh rosemary, leaves only, chopped	2
2	sprigs fresh thyme, leaves only, chopped	2
1	eggplant, sliced crosswise into rounds	1
12 oz	goat cheese (Snow Goat), cut into 2 oz (50 g) rounds	384 g
	Mixed baby greens, to serve six	
¼ cup	vinaigrette (your choice)	50 mL

In pan over medium high heat, heat olive oil; cook onions, half of garlic, and bay leaf until onions are transparent. Add white wine and vinegar. Continue cooking until confit is reduced to half. Add salt and pepper to taste.

In small bowl, combine vegetable oil, remaining garlic, balsamic vinegar, rosemary, thyme, and salt and pepper to taste. Brush this mixture onto eggplant slices and let sit for 10 minutes. Grill eggplant over high heat, turning eggplant when slightly charred, after approximately 2 minutes.

Divide onion confit evenly among slices of grilled eggplant. Spread confit over each slice; place sliced rounds of goat cheese on top. Place eggplant on baking sheet and broil under preheated broiler until light golden in color.

Place several pieces of eggplant on top of baby greens, preset and dressed on individual salad plates, forming tower shape.

Makes 6 servings.

MAKE AHEAD: **The onion confit can be prepared a day in advance, or earlier in the day.**

Grilled Portobello Mushrooms with Goat Cheese and Arugula

The fresh herbs add a wonderful bouquet of flavors to this salad.

Nutrients per serving:
Calories: 255
Protein: 6 grams
Fat: 19 grams
Carbohydrate: 15 grams

4	pieces Portobello mushrooms, medium size	4
2 tbsp	extra virgin olive oil	30 mL
1 tbsp	balsamic vinegar	15 mL
½ tsp	chopped garlic	2 mL
Pinch	salt	Pinch
1 tsp	each chopped fresh rosemary, thyme, and chives	5 mL
1	bunch arugula (rinsed with cold water)	1
¼ cup	goat cheese, crumbled	50 mL
Pinch	cracked black pepper	Pinch
4	leaves fresh basil, shredded	4

Brush portobello mushrooms with half of olive oil and grill on medium-hot grill, turning frequently. When mushrooms begin to release their water, remove them from grill and set aside to keep warm.

In mixing bowl, whisk together remaining olive oil, vinegar, garlic, salt, and herbs, except basil.

TO SERVE:
Arrange washed arugula on two plates. Toss warm mushrooms in vinaigrette and place on top of arugula. Crumble goat cheese on top and garnish around salad with black pepper and basil leaves.

Makes 2 servings.

KITCHEN POINTER: If you want to make this salad, but don't have access to a grill, sauté the mushrooms in a pan over medium heat. To save time, the vinaigrette ingredients may be added right into the pan when the mushrooms are cooked.

Black Bean Salad with Bell Peppers

This unique salad has great flavor, texture, and appearance.

Vinaigrette

½ cup	water	125 mL
4 oz	raisins, chopped	113 g
½ cup	fresh lime juice	125 mL
6 tbsp	extra virgin olive oil	100 mL
2 tbsp	dried oregano	25 mL
4 tsp	honey	20 mL
4 tsp	each ground cumin and coriander	20 mL
	Salt and pepper	

Salad

| 2 | 19-oz (540 mL) cans black beans, drained and rinsed | 2 |
| ½ cup | each chopped red pepper, yellow pepper, green pepper, red onion, and fresh parsley | 125 mL |

This recipe is FREE of the following triggers (marked ✔)

Caffeine	✔
Chocolate	✔
Citrus fruits	
Red wine	✔
Aged cheese	✔
MSG & Nitrates	✔
Aspartame	✔
Nuts	✔
Onions & Garlic	
Yeast	✔

Nutrients per serving
(when serving 8):
Calories: 308
Protein: 10 grams
Fat: 12 grams
Carbohydrate: 40 grams

Vinaigrette: In heavy saucepan, boil water and raisins for about 2 minutes. Remove from heat; cover and let stand for about an hour to soften.

Transfer raisin mixture to food processor. Add lime juice, olive oil, oregano, honey, cumin, and coriander; process until smooth. Season to taste with salt and pepper.

Salad: In large bowl, toss beans, peppers, onion, and parsley. Add enough dressing to coat. Season with salt and pepper to taste.
Makes 6 to 8 servings.

MAKE AHEAD: The salad can be made 6 hours ahead. Let stand at room temperature. The vinaigrette can be made a day ahead. Before using, let stand at room temperature.

VARIATION: A combination of different types of beans (black, red, pinto) can be used for even more interest.

Curried Chicken and Rice Salad with Almonds

Nutrients per serving:
Calories: 722
Protein: 25 grams
Fat: 26 grams
Carbohydrate: 97 grams

This flavorful dish is perfect served cold as a salad, but it can also be served hot as a main course. Worcestershire sauce sometimes contains MSG, so you should be aware of this potential trigger.

2 cups	basmati rice	500 mL
1-½ cups	cooked chicken (skinless, boneless breasts)	375 mL
2 tbsp	olive oil	25 mL
2 tbsp	plain low-fat yogurt	25 mL
1 tbsp	curry powder	15 mL
1 tbsp	light soy sauce (naturally brewed or Homemade, see p. 114)	15 mL
2 tsp	wine vinegar	10 mL
1 tsp	celery seed	5 mL
1 tsp	honey	5 mL
1 tsp	Worcestershire sauce	5 mL
½ tsp	garlic powder	2 mL
½ tsp	pepper	2 mL
1-½ cups	diced red, yellow, or orange pepper	375 mL
1 cup	slivered almonds	250 mL
½ cup	diced celery	125 mL
¼ cup	diced green onion	50 mL
	Salt and pepper	

VARIATION: **If serving the next day as a cold salad, add 1 tbsp (15 mL) plain low-fat yogurt to moisten and ¼ cup (50 mL) shredded carrot. Mix well.**

Cook basmati rice according to package instructions. Set aside.

Dice chicken. In nonstick pan, lightly sauté chicken with olive oil, yogurt, curry powder, soy sauce, wine vinegar, celery seed, honey, Worcestershire sauce, garlic powder, and pepper until cooked through.

Add basmati rice and remaining ingredients (peppers, almonds, celery, and green onion); cover and simmer about 5 minutes or until vegetables are tender. Season with salt and pepper to taste.

Makes 4 servings.

Warm Spinach Salad with Prawns

A beautiful and elegant salad bursting with nutrition and flavor.

1	**bag fresh spinach**	1
2 tbsp	**olive oil**	25 mL
8	**medium tiger prawns, cleaned**	8
1	**red pepper, cut in julienne**	1
2	**Roma tomatoes, seeded and cut in julienne**	2
¼ cup	**vinegar**	50 mL
	Salt and pepper	

Trim and wash spinach. Pat dry.

In sauté pan over medium-high heat, heat olive oil. Add prawns and cook until prawns turn red and are firm.

Add red pepper and tomatoes; cook for 1 minute longer.

Add spinach and vinegar. Remove from heat and gently toss. Season with salt and pepper to taste.

Transfer to individual salad plates and serve.

Makes 2 servings.

This recipe is FREE of the following triggers (marked ✔)

Caffeine ✔
Chocolate ✔
Citrus fruits ✔
Red wine ✔
Aged cheese ✔
MSG & Nitrates ✔
Aspartame ✔
Nuts ✔
Onions & Garlic ✔
Yeast ✔

Nutrients per serving:
Calories: 217
Protein: 11 grams
Fat: 13 grams
Carbohydrate: 14 grams

Meatless Main Courses

Roasted Wild Mushroom Veggie Burgers

Nutrients per serving:
Calories: 205
Protein: 13 grams
Fat: 9 grams
Carbohydrate: 18 grams

Made with mushrooms and tofu these are a delicious and nutritious alternative to regular beef patties.

2 tbsp	olive oil	25 mL
1	medium onion, chopped	1
Pinch	salt	Pinch
1 cup	dry shiitake mushrooms, soaked in hot water until soft	250 mL
2 cups	stemmed and chopped domestic, wild, or portobello mushrooms	500 mL
16 oz	extra-firm tofu, mashed	454 g
¾ cup	quick-cooking oats	175 mL
⅓ cup	toasted wheat germ	75 mL
⅓ cup	breadcrumbs	75 mL
2 tbsp	Worcestershire sauce	25 mL
½ tsp	garlic powder	2 mL

In large nonstick skillet, heat olive oil and sauté onions and salt for about 5 minutes.

Stem softened shiitake mushrooms. In blender or food processor, mince all the mushrooms.

Add mushroom mixture to onions in skillet and cook for about 10 minutes, stirring occasionally.

Remove mixture from heat and mix with mashed tofu. Add remaining ingredients and mix well. Measure out eight ½-cup (125-mL) portions. With wet hands form portions into patties.

Place on greased cookie sheet. Bake in 375°F (190°C) oven for 25 minutes, turning once after 15 minutes. Just before serving, heat burgers in skillet or on grill to heat through.

Makes about 8 burgers.

Pasta Salad with Red Peppers and Artichokes

This colorful and tasty main-course salad is ideal for a cold vegetarian lunch or a light supper.

1 lb	fusilli or penne	500 g
2	medium tomatoes, chopped	2
2	medium red or yellow peppers, chopped	2
1-½ cups	black olives (optional)	375 mL
¾ cup	marinated artichokes, drained and chopped	175 mL
¼ cup	grated Parmesan cheese	50 mL
⅓ cup	olive oil	75 mL
1 tbsp	red wine vinegar (or cider vinegar)	15 mL
2 tsp	Dijon mustard (or the same amount of dry mustard if MSG is a trigger)	10 mL
2 to 3	cloves garlic, peeled and minced	2 to 3
	Salt and pepper	

This recipe is FREE of the following triggers (marked ✔)

Caffeine ✔
Chocolate ✔
Citrus fruits ✔
Red wine
Aged cheese
MSG & Nitrates
Aspartame ✔
Nuts ✔
Onions & Garlic
Yeast ✔

Bring large pot of water to boil. Add pasta and cook until just tender. Drain and place in large mixing bowl.

Add tomatoes, peppers, olives (if using), artichokes, and Parmesan cheese to pasta and toss together.

Dressing: In small bowl, whisk together olive oil, vinegar, mustard, and garlic.

Toss pasta with dressing. Season with salt and pepper to taste and serve.

Makes 4 to 6 servings.

Nutrients per serving:
Calories: 463
Protein: 13 grams
Fat: 15 grams
Carbohydrate: 69 grams

Chinese Noodle Salad with Roasted Eggplant

This recipe is FREE of the following triggers (marked ✔)
Caffeine ✔
Chocolate ✔
Citrus fruits ✔
Red wine ✔
Aged cheese ✔
MSG & Nitrates ✔
Aspartame ✔
Nuts ✔
Onions & Garlic
Yeast ✔

Nutrients per serving:
Calories: 577
Protein: 16 grams
Fat: 25 grams
Carbohydrate: 72 grams

Here's an elegant dish that combines exciting flavors and textures. Mung beans can be found in Asian supermarkets.

Marinade and Noodles

½ cup	dark sesame oil	125 mL
½ cup	soy sauce, naturally brewed or Homemade (see p. 114)	125 mL
3 to 4 tbsp	sugar	45 to 60 mL
3 tbsp	balsamic vinegar	50 mL
3 tbsp	coriander, chopped	50 mL
8 to 10	scallions, thinly sliced	8 to 10
1 tbsp	red pepper oil	15 mL
2-½ tsp	salt	12 mL
1	15-oz (435-g) package chinese egg noddles (thinnest available) or linguine	1

Eggplant and Vegetable Garnishes

1 lb	firm, shiny Japanese eggplants	500 g
1 tbsp	fresh ginger, peeled and minced	15 mL
1	clove garlic, chopped	1
1 tsp	salt	5 mL
1 cup	blanched snow peas, string removed, cut into thin strips	250 mL
½ lb	mung beans	250 g
3 tbsp	sesame seeds (optional)	50 mL
1	medium carrot, peeled, julienned	1
	Coriander for garnish	

MARINADE AND NOODLES:

In large bowl, combine all ingredients (except noodles).

Stir marinade mixture until sugar dissolves.

Bring large pot of unsalted water to boil. Gently pull apart strands of noodles, loosening and fluffing; add them to boiling water. Cook noodles until just tender, about 3 minutes. Drain and place in mixing bowl. Stir marinade; pour half on noodles and toss. Set remaining marinade aside.

EGGPLANT AND VEGETABLE GARNISHES:
Preheat oven to 400°F (200°C). In baking dish, pierce eggplants and bake until soft, about 20 minutes, depending on size, turning once; let cool. Slice lengthwise; peel skin. Shred eggplant into ¼-inch (5-mm) strips.

Add ginger and garlic to reserved marinade. Add eggplant strips to mixture, turning them over several times. Set aside.

Bring quart (1 L) of water to boil and add salt. Blanch snow peas; rinse in cold water and cut into strips. Blanch mung beans and rinse. Lay to dry on towel.

In frying pan, roast sesame seeds until lightly colored and fragrant.

Toss noodles with eggplant strips and half of sesame seeds.

Mound noodles on platter; distribute carrots, snow peas, and mung bean sprouts over noodles and garnish with remaining sesame seeds and coriander.

Makes 4 to 6 servings.

VARIATIONS: **Substitute sesame seeds with roasted peanuts or cashews. Blanched asparagus tips can be used instead of eggplants. Long red or white radishes, thinly sliced, then slivered, can also be included as a garnish.**

Vegetable and Cheese Lasagna

A tasty dish that's easy when you use ready-made marinara sauce. If MSG is a trigger, make sure you choose the appropriate variety of sauce. This sauce may also contain onion, so read the label carefully.

1 cup	prepared marinara sauce	250 mL
1 cup	coarsely chopped plum tomatoes	250 mL
1	medium zucchini, thinly sliced	1
¼ cup	chopped fresh basil leaves or	50 mL
	1 tbsp (15 mL) dried	
1 cup	ricotta cheese	250 mL
⅔ cup	grated Parmesan cheese	175 mL
	Salt and pepper	
3	lasagna noodles	3
	Additional grated Parmesan cheese	

Nutrients per serving:
Calories: 529
Protein: 33 grams
Fat: 25 grams
Carbohydrate: 43 grams

In heavy saucepan over medium heat, simmer marinara sauce, tomatoes, zucchini, and basil about 8 minutes or until zucchini is tender, stirring occasionally.

In bowl, mix ricotta and ½ cup (175 mL) Parmesan to blend. Season with salt and pepper to taste.

In pot of boiling salted water cook lasagna noodles until just tender. Drain. Cut in half, crosswise, to make 6 pieces.

Set aside 2 tbsp (25 mL) vegetable sauce for topping. Place 2 noodle pieces in greased 8-inch (2 L) square glass baking dish. Spread ¼ of cheese mixture, then ¼ sauce over each noodle. Repeat. Finish with two noodle pieces, reserved sauce, and remaining Parmesan.

Bake at 375°F (190°C), uncovered, for about 15 minutes or until hot and bubbling. Serve with additional Parmesan cheese.

Makes 2 servings.

VARIATION: You can make this with whatever vegetables you have on hand; for example, mushrooms, spinach, and onions could easily be substituted.

Opposite: Pumpkin Bisque (p. 45)
Overleaf: Warmed Goat Cheese Salad with Grilled Vegetables (p. 52)

Grilled Portobello Mushrooms with Asparagus and Herbed Polenta

In this hearty dish, the polenta is herbed and eaten soft.

6	medium Portobello mushrooms	6
4 tsp	extra virgin olive oil	20 mL
1	bunch asparagus, washed and peeled	1
8 cups	salted water	2 L
1 lb	instant polenta	500 g
2 tbsp	unsalted butter	25 mL
1 tbsp	each fresh rosemary, thyme, and parsley, chopped	15 mL
	Salt and freshly ground pepper	

This recipe is FREE of the following triggers (marked ✔)

Caffeine ✔
Chocolate ✔
Citrus fruits ✔
Red wine ✔
Aged cheese ✔
MSG & Nitrates ✔
Aspartame ✔
Nuts ✔
Onions & Garlic ✔
Yeast ✔

Clean mushrooms and brush with 3 tsp (15 mL) of olive oil. Season with salt and pepper to taste.

In large skillet of boiling salted water, cook asparagus for 2 to 3 minutes. Remove asparagus and refresh by plunging into bowl filled with iced cold water. Drain and allow asparagus to dry by placing on pan or plate lined with paper towels.

Grill asparagus and mushrooms over medium heat for 2 to 4 minutes or until just tender; watch carefully.

In large saucepan of boiling salted water, add 1 tsp (5 mL) olive oil and polenta; cook for 6 minutes over medium heat.

Remove polenta from heat and stir in butter and herbs until smooth.

To serve, spoon polenta onto platter and arrange asparagus and mushrooms. Season with freshly ground pepper, if desired.

Makes 6 servings.

Nutrients per serving:
Calories: 372
Protein: 8 grams
Fat: 8 grams
Carbohydrate: 67 grams

MAKE AHEAD:
The polenta can be prepared earlier and warmed just prior to serving.

Opposite: Baked Halibut with Dill Crust and Red Pepper Sauce (p. 93)
Overleaf: Curried Chicken with Peaches and Coconut (p. 69)

Stir-Fried Fresh Vegetables and Tofu

This recipe is FREE of the following triggers (marked ✔)

Caffeine	✔
Chocolate	✔
Citrus fruits	✔
Red wine	✔
Aged cheese	✔
MSG & Nitrates	✔
Aspartame	✔
Nuts	✔
Onions & Garlic	
Yeast	✔

Nutrients per serving:
Calories: 490
Protein: 18 grams
Fat: 30 grams
Carbohydrate: 32 grams

This stir fry can be made with or without the tofu. Either way, the simple sauce adds an excellent flavor. Serve the stir fry over rice for a complete meal.

6 tbsp	olive oil	90 mL
8 oz	firm tofu, well drained, cut into ½-inch (1 cm) cubes	250 g
2 tbsp	peeled and minced fresh ginger	25 mL
3	cloves garlic, minced	3
1 lb	fresh shiitake mushrooms, stems trimmed, caps sliced	500 g
2 cups	broccoli florets	500 mL
2	red peppers, cut into strips	2
2	bunches green onions, cut into 1-inch (2.5 cm) pieces	2
½ cup	dry white wine	125 mL
¼ cup	soy sauce, naturally brewed or Homemade (see p. 114)	50 mL
1 tbsp	sesame oil	15 mL
	Salt and pepper	

In large nonstick skillet or wok, heat 3 tbsp (45 mL) of olive oil over high heat. Add tofu and stir gently for about 4 minutes until it starts to brown around edges. Transfer to bowl.

To skillet, add remaining oil, ginger, and garlic and stir for about 1 minute. Add mushrooms and stir-fry for about 5 minutes or until tender around edges. Add broccoli, red peppers, and green onions; stir-fry for about 3 minutes or until just tender. Add tofu to vegetable mixture in skillet and mix. Add white wine, soy sauce, and sesame oil. Simmer for about 1 minute or until heated through.

Before serving, season with salt and pepper to taste.

Makes 4 servings.

Meat and Poultry

Homestyle Chicken and Rice Casserole

This is comfort food at its tastiest and easiest.

2 cups	cooked, chopped chicken	500 mL
2 cups	uncooked rice	500 mL
2	10-oz (284 mL) cans cream of mushroom soup (without MSG) or homemade, p. 43	284 mL
1 cup	water	250 mL
5	green onions, chopped	5
3 tsp	curry powder	15 mL
2 tsp	salt	10 mL
1 tsp	sage	5 mL
½ tsp	pepper	2 mL

In large bowl, mix all ingredients, stirring well. Pour into 3 qt (3 L) casserole dish. Bake in 325°F (160°C) oven for 2 hours or until liquid is absorbed and rice is tender.

Makes 4 to 6 servings.

VARIATION: Try adding ½ cup (125 mL) chopped broccoli before baking for something a little different.

This recipe is FREE of the following triggers (marked ✔)

| Caffeine ✔ |
| Chocolate ✔ |
| Citrus fruits ✔ |
| Red wine ✔ |
| Aged cheese ✔ |
| MSG & Nitrates |
| Aspartame ✔ |
| Nuts ✔ |
| Onions & Garlic |
| Yeast ✔ |

Nutrients per serving (when recipe serves 6):
Calories: 389
Protein: 16 grams
Fat: 9 grams
Carbohydrate: 61 grams

Simple Chicken Kiev

Nutrients per serving:
Calories: 278
Protein: 32 grams
Fat: 10 grams
Carbohydrate: 15 grams

This recipe turns a complicated old-world dish into a tasty and easy-to-prepare modern-day delight. Serve it with rice.

4	boneless, skinless chicken breasts	4
	Salt and pepper	
4 tsp	margarine	20 mL
4 tsp	chopped chives	20 mL
½ tsp	tarragon	2 mL
2	eggs	2
2 tsp	water	10 mL
¼ cup	all-purpose flour	50 mL
½ cup	dry breadcrumbs	125 mL

Sprinkle each chicken breast with salt and pepper. Place 1 tsp (5 mL) margarine on each breast and top with 1 tsp (5 mL) chives and pinch tarragon. Fold the chicken to enclose the filling completely and secure with toothpicks.

In small bowl, beat eggs and water. Coat chicken with flour and then dip into egg mixture. Coat with breadcrumbs. Place chicken seam-side up into greased baking pan.

Bake in 400°F (200°C) oven for 20 minutes, turning once, or until juices run clear when chicken is pierced with fork.

Makes 4 servings.

Curried Chicken with Peaches and Coconut

For a simple accompaniment, serve this chicken dish with basmati rice.

2 tbsp	butter	25 mL
1 tbsp	oil	15 mL
3-½ lb	frying chicken, cut into pieces	1.75 kg
2 tbsp	chopped onion (omit onion if a trigger)	25 mL
1	small clove garlic, chopped (omit if a trigger)	1
1 cup	diced peaches, fresh or tinned (drained, if tinned)	250 mL
⅔ cup	chicken stock (see p. XX)	150 mL
1-½ tsp	curry powder	7 mL
½ tsp	cumin	2 mL
¼ tsp	brown sugar	1 mL
	Salt and pepper	
	Peach slices	
	Shredded coconut to garnish	

This recipe is FREE of the following triggers (marked ✔)

Caffeine ✔
Chocolate ✔
Citrus fruits ✔
Red wine ✔
Aged cheese ✔
MSG & Nitrates ✔
Aspartame ✔
Nuts ✔
Onions & Garlic
Yeast ✔

Nutrients per serving (when recipe serves 6):
Calories: 397
Protein: 33 grams
Fat: 25 grams
Carbohydrate: 10 grams

In large skillet, heat butter and oil over medium-high heat. Add chicken pieces; brown slowly on all sides. Remove from pan.

Add onion and garlic and cook 4 to 5 minutes or until onion is transparent. Add diced peaches; cook, stirring, until mixture is well combined, about 2 minutes.

Meanwhile in bowl, combine stock, curry powder, cumin, and brown sugar. Add to skillet and heat 5 minutes.

Return chicken to skillet and season with salt and pepper to taste. Cover and simmer until tender, about 25 to 30 minutes. Remove chicken from sauce and place on heated serving platter and keep warm.

Add sliced peaches to sauce. Cook just until glazed; pour sauce over chicken. Garnish with coconut.

Makes 4 to 6 servings.

Japanese-Glazed Chicken

Nutrients per serving:
Calories: 480
Protein: 36 grams
Fat: 8 grams
Carbohydrate: 66 grams

This delectable dish is perfect for an Asian-inspired meal. Serve it with rice and mixed vegetables.

8	boneless skinless chicken thighs	8
1	egg	1
1 cup	milk	250 mL
1-½ cups	all-purpose flour	375 mL
½ cup	granulated sugar	125 mL
½ cup	vinegar	125 mL
3 tbsp	water	50 mL
3 tbsp	soy sauce, naturally brewed or Homemade (see p. 114)	50 mL
1 tsp	salt	5 mL

Trim excess fat from chicken thighs. In bowl, mix egg and milk. Dip each chicken piece in egg/milk mixture and coat in flour. In frying pan over medium heat, brown chicken lightly on both sides, approximately 2 to 3 minutes per side.

Meanwhile, in medium-sized bowl, combine remaining ingredients. When chicken is browned, arrange in 13- x 9-inch (3.5 L) pan (glass preferably); pour soy mixture over top. Bake in 350°F (180°C) oven for 1 hour, basting chicken with pan juices every 15 minutes.

Makes 4 servings.

Pasta with Chicken, Asparagus, and Sweet Red Pepper

The Dijon and rosemary give this pasta dish a beautifully mellow flavor.

2 cups	bowtie (farfalle) pasta	500 mL
2	boneless skinless chicken breasts	2
1	bunch asparagus	1
1	sweet red pepper	1
3 tbsp	olive oil	50 mL
2 tbsp	Dijon mustard (or the same amount of dry mustard if MSG is a trigger)	25 mL
1 tbsp	chopped garlic	15 mL
1 tbsp	chopped fresh rosemary	15 mL
½ cup	dry white wine (optional)	125 mL
1 cup	35% whipping cream	250 mL
	Salt and pepper	

This recipe is FREE of the following triggers (marked ✔)

Caffeine	✔
Chocolate	✔
Citrus fruits	✔
Red wine	✔
Aged cheese	✔
MSG & Nitrates	
Aspartame	✔
Nuts	✔
Onions & Garlic	
Yeast	✔

In large pot of boiling salted water, cook pasta until tender but firm, approximately 6 to 8 minutes. Drain and set aside.

Cut chicken into bite-size pieces and set aside.

Wash and cut asparagus into 1-inch (2.5 cm) pieces and set aside.

Cut red pepper in half; remove seeds and cut lengthwise into thin strips (julienne). Set aside.

In medium frying pan, heat oil over medium heat; add chicken and cook for approximately 5 minutes. Add asparagus and continue cooking for another 2 minutes. Add Dijon mustard, garlic, rosemary, julienned red peppers and cook for 1 minute.

Add dry white wine (if using) and allow to reduce by half. Add whipping cream and reduce until mixture begins to thicken. Season to taste with salt and pepper.

Add pasta and stir until thoroughly mixed and pasta is reheated. Serve immediately.

Makes 2 to 4 servings.

Nutrients per serving:
Calories: 538
Protein: 22 grams
Fat: 34 grams
Carbohydrate: 36 grams

Chicken Kabobs with Homemade Barbecue Sauce

The deep and mellow flavor of the barbecue sauce makes it the perfect accompaniment to grilled chicken. Serve these kabobs on a bed of steamed rice. Many brands of mustard and ketchup contain MSG, so watch for these potential triggers.

This recipe is FREE of the following triggers (marked ✔)
Caffeine ✔
Chocolate ✔
Citrus fruits ✔
Red wine ✔
Aged cheese ✔
MSG & Nitrates
Aspartame ✔
Nuts ✔
Onions & Garlic
Yeast ✔

Nutrients per serving:
Calories: 167
Protein: 28 grams
Fat: 3 grams
Carbohydrate: 7 grams

Barbecue Sauce

6	cloves garlic, crushed	6
1	medium onion, chopped	1
1 cup	ketchup	250 mL
¼ cup	water	50 mL
¼ cup	maple syrup	50 mL
3 tbsp	Dijon mustard (or same amount of dry mustard if MSG is a trigger)	50 mL
3 tbsp	balsamic vinegar	50 mL
2 tbsp	molasses	25 mL
1 tsp	each chopped fresh thyme, rosemary, basil, marjoram, and oregano	5 mL
1 tsp	ground cumin	5 mL

Kabobs

10	boneless skinless chicken breasts (each breast cut in ½ lengthwise, then each strip in 3- to 5-oz/75 to 125 g pieces)	10
1	each red, yellow, and green pepper, each cut into 20 ½-inch (1 cm) square pieces	1

BARBECUE SAUCE:

In bowl, combine all ingredients. Set aside.

KABOBS:

Marinate diced chicken breast in 1 cup (250 mL) of barbecue sauce overnight. Soak 20 wooden bamboo skewers in water overnight.

Skewer chicken and peppers onto bamboo skewers, alternating chicken with different color pepper. Make 20 kabobs, allowing 2 per person.

On preheated barbecue, grill kabobs for 3 to 5 minutes per side or until chicken is no longer pink inside. Baste with sauce as required during grilling.

Serve brochettes on bed of steamed rice.

Makes 10 servings.

MAKE AHEAD: **The barbecue sauce can be made 2 days in advance, while the kabobs can be prepared a day in advance. Store in the refrigerator until ready to grill.**

Poached Chicken with Wild Rice and Baby Vegetables

Nutrients per serving:
Calories: 603
Protein: 37 grams
Fat: 27 grams
Carbohydrate: 53 grams

* The wild rice must be soaked for at least 6 hours in fresh, cold water before cooking.

The rich and creamy sauce makes this dish elegant enough for company.

1 cup	mix of wild* and long grain rice	250 mL
4 cups	chicken stock (see p. 111)	1 L
4	boneless skinless chicken breasts	4
3	celery stalks, sliced into 1-inch (2.5 cm) long sticks	3
2	parsnips, peeled and sliced into 1/4-inch (5 mm) rounds	2
1	carrot, peeled and sliced into 1/4-inch (5 mm) rounds	1
1	bunch Swiss chard, washed and coarsely chopped	1
1 cup	35% cream	250 mL
	Salt and pepper	
1	bunch Italian parsley, coarsely chopped	1

In ovenproof pot with lid, cover wild and long grain rice mixture with chicken stock to about 1 inch (2.5 cm) above rice. Bake, covered, in preheated 450°F (230°C) oven for about 35 minutes. Remove and let stand for 15 minutes.

In stewing pot, arrange chicken and vegetables. Cover with remaining chicken stock and bring to boil over medium heat.

Reduce heat to maintain simmer and cook for about 10 minutes.

Remove chicken and vegetables from stock, keeping warm and covered until serving time. Bring chicken stock to boil once more; add cream. Stir frequently until sauce becomes thick enough to coat spoon. Season with salt and pepper to taste.

To serve, spoon rice onto serving dish or individual plates, creating bed. Place chicken and vegetables on top of rice. Garnish with parsley and serve.

Makes 4 servings.

Roast Duck with Spiced Honey

The succulent flavor of roast duck is combined with the sweet goodness of honey and spice in this elegant entree, perfect for entertaining.

2	ducks (each 4 to 5 lb/2 to 2.5 kg), cut in half lengthwise	2
	Salt and pepper	
½ cup	honey	125 mL
1 tbsp	cumin	15 mL
1 tbsp	ground fennel seed	15 mL

Preheat oven to 450°F (230°C).

Place duck halves skin side down on cutting board. Trim any excess fat to edge of skin. Generously season inside and outside of duck halves with salt and pepper.

Place duck halves, breast side up, on roasting rack set in shallow baking pan. Roast in preheated oven for 20 minutes. Reduce heat to 375°F (190°C) and continue roasting for another 20 minutes.

Meanwhile, in small bowl, mix honey with cumin and fennel seed to form baste.

Remove duck halves from oven and baste with honey-spice mixture. Return duck halves to oven and cook for additional 20 minutes or until skin appears crisp.

Makes 4 to 6 servings.

KITCHEN POINTER: **Cooking times may vary depending upon size and weight of duck. Check with your butcher to verify appropriate cooking times.**

This recipe is FREE of the following triggers (marked ✔)

Caffeine ✔	
Chocolate ✔	
Citrus fruits ✔	
Red wine ✔	
Aged cheese ✔	
MSG & Nitrates ✔	
Aspartame ✔	
Nuts ✔	
Onions & Garlic ✔	
Yeast ✔	

Nutrients per serving (when recipe serves 6):
Calories: 902
Protein: 48 grams
Fat: 70 grams
Carbohydrate: 20 grams

Phyllo-Wrapped Chicken with Mushrooms and Spinach in Citron Vodka Sauce

This recipe is FREE of the following triggers (marked ✔)

Caffeine	✔
Chocolate	✔
Citrus fruits	
Red wine	✔
Aged cheese	✔
MSG & Nitrates	✔
Aspartame	✔
Nuts	✔
Onions & Garlic	
Yeast	✔

Nutrients per serving:
Calories: 531
Protein: 22 grams
Fat: 35 grams
Carbohydrate: 32 grams

Want to try something different? This classic recipe combines the delicate flavors of chicken, mushrooms, and spinach with the zesty taste of lemon. If lemon juice is a trigger, try using extra amounts of lemon grass.

1	pkg fresh spinach, trimmed	1
2	boneless skinless chicken breasts, lightly pounded	2
1 cup	sliced button mushrooms	250 mL
¼ cup	melted butter or oil	50 mL
1 cup	cooked rice	250 mL
4	sheets phyllo pastry	4
Pinch	salt	Pinch

Sauce

1 cup	35% cream	250 mL
½ cup	chicken stock (see p. 111)	125 mL
1 tsp	lemon juice	5 mL
1 tsp	lemon grass, finely chopped (optional) (available at oriental markets and most supermarkets)	5 mL
1 oz	Citron Vodka (optional)	25 mL
	Salt	

Wash spinach; shake off excess water and place in saucepan. With just water clinging to leaves, cook spinach, uncovered, until wilted. Drain, squeeze excess moisture from spinach and chop.

In large skillet, sauté chicken breasts until seared outside. Remove and let cool slightly.

In skillet, sauté mushrooms in oil or butter. Add rice and chopped spinach to mushrooms. Let cool slightly.

Brush one phyllo sheet with butter (or oil). Place second sheet on top and brush lightly with butter (or oil). Fold in half.

Divide spinach mixture in two. Place in pile on phyllo. Place chicken breast on top and fold together. Repeat with remaining chicken breast.

Bake at 400°F (200°C) for about 15 to 20 minutes or until chicken is no longer pink inside and pastry is golden brown.

Meanwhile, in saucepan, bring sauce ingredients to boil; let simmer a few minutes until lightly thickened.

Add vodka to sauce, if using.

Season with salt to taste. If lemon grass is unavailable, use basil, thyme, or mixture of lemon zest and thyme. To serve, place generous amount of sauce on individual plates; place phyllo-wrapped chicken in center of each plate.

Makes 4 servings.

MAKE AHEAD: Follow the recipe and wrap the chicken in the phyllo earlier in the day; wrap tightly with plastic wrap and store in the refrigerator. Bake just before serving time.

Swedish Meatballs

This classic dish is a wonderful combination of spiced beef in a creamy sauce. Serve with rice or noodles, a crisp green salad, and crusty bread to mop up the sauce.

Nutrients per serving (when recipe serves 8):
Calories: 564
Protein: 31 grams
Fat: 40 grams
Carbohydrate: 20 grams

1 cup	fine breadcrumbs	250 mL
2-½ cups	milk	625 mL
2 lbs	lean ground beef	1 kg
2	eggs, lightly beaten	2
1-½ tsp	salt	7 mL
¼ tsp	pepper	1 mL
1 tsp	nutmeg	5 mL
½ cup	butter or margarine	125 mL
¼ cup	all-purpose flour	50 mL
3 cups	beef stock (see p. 111)	750 mL
1-½ cups	light cream	375 mL

In large bowl, soften breadcrumbs in 1 cup (250 mL) of the milk. Add beef, eggs, and seasonings; mix well. Shape into 1-inch (2.5 cm) balls. In large skillet, brown meatballs in butter all over. Remove from skillet and set aside.

In same skillet, add flour to skillet drippings and blend well. Gradually add stock, remaining milk, and cream to flour mixture and cook over low heat, stirring constantly, for about 3 minutes.

Add meatballs to sauce and simmer for 10 to 15 minutes or until heated through, stirring occasionally. Transfer to covered dish and serve.

Makes 6 to 8 servings.

Sweet and Sour Pork Chops

This tangy dish is delicious served with potatoes and spinach.

¾ cup	water	175 mL
½ cup	brown sugar	125 mL
½ cup	ketchup	125 mL
½ cup	white vinegar	125 mL
2 tbsp	Worcestershire sauce	25 mL
1 tsp	chili powder	5 mL
4 to 6	pork chops	4 to 6
2	medium onions, sliced	2

In large bowl, mix water, sugar, ketchup, vinegar, Worcestershire sauce, and chili powder.

Place pork chops in roasting pan and cover with sliced onions.

Pour sauce mixture over pork chops and onions. Cover and cook in 300°F (150°C) oven for about 1 to 1-½ hours or until chops are tender.

Makes 4 servings.

This recipe is FREE of the following triggers (marked ✔)

Caffeine ✔
Chocolate ✔
Citrus fruits ✔
Red wine ✔
Aged cheese ✔
MSG & Nitrates
Aspartame ✔
Nuts ✔
Onions & Garlic
Yeast ✔

Nutrients per serving:
Calories: 329
Protein: 22 grams
Fat: 9 grams
Carbohydrate: 40 grams

Pork Tenderloin with Fresh Tomato Sauce

Nutrients per serving:
Calories: 680
Protein: 44 grams
Fat: 12 grams
Carbohydrate: 99 grams

These tender pieces of pork cook quickly and are a perfect accompaniment to this savory tomato-based sauce.

2 tbsp	olive oil	25 mL
1 lb	pork tenderloin, cubed	500 g
½ cup	green pepper, coarsely chopped	125 mL
1	clove garlic, chopped	1
1	celery stalk, coarsely chopped	1
2 cups	seeded and chopped tomatoes	500 mL
½ tsp	each fresh thyme, oregano, and basil	2 mL
	Salt and pepper	
1 lb	fettuccine	500 g

In large skillet over medium-high heat, heat olive oil. Sauté pork until brown. Remove and set aside, keeping warm.

In same pan, cook pepper, garlic, and celery until tender. Add tomatoes, thyme, oregano, and basil and simmer for 15 minutes longer.

Return pork to pan and cook for another 4 to 6 minutes. Season with salt and pepper to taste.

Meanwhile, in large pot of boiling salted water, cook fettuccine until al dente.

Drain pasta and serve with pork mixture over top. Garnish, if desired, with sprig of thyme or basil.

Makes 4 servings.

Quick Lamb Patties

Served with new potatoes and asparagus, these mint-flavored patties make a great meal. Chutney may contain citrus fruits or MSG, so watch for these potential triggers.

10 oz	ground lamb	284 g
1	green onion, finely chopped	1
1	clove garlic, finely chopped	1
2 tbsp	minced fresh mint	25 mL
	Salt and pepper	
3 tbsp	chutney	50 mL

Preheat broiler. In small bowl, combine lamb with green onion, garlic, and mint. Season with salt and pepper to taste. Mix well.

Shape lamb mixture into 2 patties, each about 1 inch (2.5 cm) thick.

Under broiler, broil patties for about 4 minutes or until brown. Turn patties over and broil for about another 4 minutes or until desired doneness and browned.

Spread half of chutney on each pattie. Continue broiling for about 1 minute or until chutney begins to bubble. Transfer patties to plates.

Makes 2 servings.

This recipe is FREE of the following triggers (marked ✔)

Caffeine ✔
Chocolate ✔
Citrus fruits
Red wine ✔
Aged cheese ✔
MSG & Nitrates ✔
Aspartame ✔
Nuts ✔
Onions & Garlic
Yeast ✔

Nutrients per serving:
Calories: 309
Protein: 27 grams
Fat: 21 grams
Carbohydrate: 3 grams

Honey-Roasted Lamb Tenderloin with Green Asparagus and Plantain Mash

Delectable pieces of lamb are combined with a honey glaze and mixed with fresh green asparagus and the succulent flavor of roasted plantain.

2 tbsp	honey	25 mL
2 tbsp	balsamic vinegar	25 mL
4	lamb tenderloins	4
2	ripe plantain, skinned and chopped	2
1 tsp	olive oil	5 mL
	Salt and pepper	
¼ cup	vegetable stock (see p. 110)	50 mL
1 cup	35% cream, reduced by half	250 mL
2 tbsp	vegetable oil	25 mL
30	spears asparagus, cut about 4 inches (10 cm) in length	30

Nutrients per serving:
Calories: 355
Protein: 18 grams
Fat: 15 grams
Carbohydrate: 37 grams

In small bowl, mix honey and balsamic vinegar. Coat lamb with this mixture and marinate for 1 to 2 hours.

Preheat oven to 400°F (200°C). In shallow roasting pan, toss plantain with olive oil and salt and pepper to taste. Cover with aluminum foil and roast in oven for 10 minutes.

Add vegetable stock to plantain (reserve a bit of stock for mashing stage). Continue roasting for 5 to 7 minutes or until plantain is very soft. Remove from oven.

In electric mixer on medium-high speed, mix plantain until mashed. Reduce speed and add cream in steady stream. Add any extra vegetable stock if mash is too thick. Keep warm.

Remove lamb from marinade; sprinkle with salt and pepper. In non-stick pan heat oil over medium-high heat. Sear lamb on all 4 sides for about 2 minutes per side.

Remove lamb and keep warm. Drain most of fat from pan and sear asparagus for about 2 minutes, stirring occasionally, until bright green and tender.

To serve, portion lamb, asparagus, and plantain mash onto individual dinner plates.

Makes 4 servings.

KITCHEN POINTER: Lamb tenderloins are usually available frozen, 8 to a package. They are not large, so 2 per person makes a reasonable portion size. If you are preparing 8 tenderloins, remember to double the amounts.

MAKE AHEAD: The plantain mash can be made earlier in the day. Keep covered. Once cooled, put in the refrigerator until needed. Reheat before serving.

Fish and Seafood

Yellowfin Tuna with Maple Mustard Sauce and Coriander Oil

Do you want to test your culinary skills? This sophisticated recipe uses raw fish and requires that you build towers!

Nutrients per serving
(when recipe serves 4):
Calories: 699
Protein: 30 grams
Fat: 55 grams
Carbohydrate: 21 grams

Coriander Oil

½ cup	chopped fresh coriander	125 mL
2 tbsp	chopped fresh parsley	25 mL
½ cup	olive oil	125 mL

Maple Mustard Sauce

2 tbsp	Dijon mustard, (or same amount of dry mustard, if MSG is a trigger)	25 mL
1 tbsp	maple syrup	15 mL
1 tbsp	fresh lemon juice	15 mL
2 tsp	sherry vinegar	10 mL
¼ cup	grape seed or vegetable oil	50 mL

Yellowfin Tuna

1	avocado, peeled, pitted, and diced	1
2 tbsp	lemon juice	25 mL
	Salt and pepper	
1	mango, peeled, pitted, and diced	1
2 tbsp	coriander oil (ingredients above, method follows)	30 mL
2	plum tomatoes, seeded and chopped	2
4 oz	yellowfin tuna, thinly diced	125 g
2 tbsp	finely chopped onions	25 mL
1 tsp	each mirin and tamari (optional) (available at specialty food shops)	5 mL
3 tbsp	chives, chopped	50 mL
1 cup	frise lettuce	250 mL
4 tsp	yellow caviar (salmon roe)	20 mL
2	6 oz (170 g) yellowfin tuna (center cut)	2

CORIANDER OIL:

In small pot of boiling salted water, blanch coriander and parsley for 30 to 60 seconds until bright green. Drain, plunge into cold water, and drain again. Dry in salad spinner or with paper towels.

In blender, puree coriander and parsley until smooth. In steady stream, add oil and blend for 3 to 4 minutes. Pass through fine sieve or cheesecloth and set aside.

MAPLE MUSTARD EMULSION:

In measuring cup or small bowl, whisk together mustard, maple syrup, lemon juice, and sherry vinegar. Still whisking, drizzle in oil. Set aside.

YELLOWFIN TUNA:

In small bowl, mix together avocado, lemon juice, and salt and pepper to taste.

In another small bowl, stir together mango, 1 tbsp (15 mL) coriander oil, and salt and pepper to taste.

In another bowl, mix tomatoes with 1 tbsp (15 mL) coriander oil and salt and pepper to taste.

Toss together diced fish, onions, mirin, tamari (if using), chives, and salt and pepper to taste.

TO ASSEMBLE:

Using a 3-inch (8 cm) round cookie cutter, build tower in center of dinner plate by packing quarter of avocado mixture into ring, followed by quarter each of mango, tomato, and fish mixtures. Pack lightly and gently remove ring.

Top each tower with equal amounts of frise; place dollop of caviar on top of each.

Arrange fish pieces around tower; drizzle plate with remaining coriander oil and maple mustard.

Makes 2 to 4 servings.

KITCHEN POINTER: Mirin is a fermented rice wine with a trace of alcohol. Tamari is a gourmet soy sauce.

MAKE AHEAD: Towers can be made 1 hour or more ahead, covered with plastic wrap, and refrigerated. Yellowfin tuna can be substituted with salmon or salmon trout.

Easy Tuna Casserole

Nutrients per serving (when recipe serves 4):
Calories: 334
Protein: 18 grams
Fat: 10 grams
Carbohydrate: 43 grams

Here's a quick recipe using ingredients from the pantry and leftover cooked rice or pasta.

2 cups	cooked rice or pasta	500 mL
1	can (6-½ oz/184 g) water-packed tuna, drained	1
2 tbsp	butter	25 mL
1	stalk celery	1
2 tbsp	all-purpose flour	25 mL
2-½ cups	milk	625 mL
½ tsp	dillweed	2 mL
	Salt and pepper	
10	soda crackers, crushed	10

In greased baking dish, combine rice (or pasta) and tuna.

In saucepan, melt butter; cook celery until transparent; stir in flour until well-combined.

Gradually add milk and stir until thickened. Add dillweed and salt and pepper to taste.

Pour sauce over tuna mixture. Top with crushed soda crackers.

Bake in 350°F (180°C) oven for 15 minutes or until bubbly around edges.

Makes 2 to 4 servings.

Herb-Crusted Salmon Fillets

The piquant-flavored crust of capers, horseradish, and fresh herbs pairs wonderfully with the mellow richness of roasted salmon. Horseradish is in the onion family, though, so watch for this potential trigger.

2 tbsp	Italian parsley, leaves only	25 mL
2 tbsp	chopped chives	25 mL
1 tbsp	capers	15 mL
1 tbsp	fresh tarragon, leaves only	15 mL
2 tsp	Dijon mustard (or same amount of dry mustard, if MSG is a trigger)	10 mL
2 tsp	Worcestershire sauce (optional)	10 mL
1 cup	fresh breadcrumbs from white bread, finely crumbled	250 mL
2 tbsp	fresh horseradish, peeled and grated	25 mL
	Salt and pepper	
4	6 oz (170 g) salmon fillets	4

This recipe is FREE of the following triggers (marked ✔)

Caffeine ✔
Chocolate ✔
Citrus fruits ✔
Red wine ✔
Aged cheese ✔
MSG & Nitrates
Aspartame ✔
Nuts ✔
Onions & Garlic
Yeast

Nutrients per serving:
Calories: 416
Protein: 37 grams
Fat: 20 grams
Carbohydrate: 22 grams

In food processor, combine parsley, chives, capers, tarragon, Dijon, and Worcestershire sauce and process for about 2 minutes or until smooth.

Transfer puree to mixing bowl. Add breadcrumbs, horseradish, and salt and pepper to taste.

Mix until well combined. Mixture should be moist, but should hold together when you squeeze it. If it is too wet, add more breadcrumbs. If too dry, add water.

Preheat oven to 400°F (200°C). Place fillets on lightly oiled baking sheet. Pack ¼ cup of mixture onto each fillet so that surface is covered and herb mix is about ½ inch (1 cm) thick. Bake for 15 minutes or until fish flakes easily when tested with fork (less if you prefer salmon slightly rare).

Makes 4 servings.

MAKE AHEAD: The herb breadcrumb mixture can be prepared earlier in the day. If you would like a more generous crust, double the amounts for the herb breadcrumb mixture.

Poached Salmon in Rosé

**Nutrients per serving
(with 2 tbsp/25 mL
Hollandaise Sauce):**
Calories: 330
Protein: 33 grams
Fat: 22 grams
Carbohydrate: trace

VARIATION: **You
can substitute
salmon with red
snapper.**

*Nothing could be more elegant than whole salmon poached in fragrant rosé
and served with Hollandaise Sauce.*

4 cups	water	1 L
¼ cup	chopped shallots	50 mL
1	stalk celery with leaves, chopped	1
1	carrot, chopped	1
1	bunch fresh parsley	1
1 tsp	salt	5 mL
2-½ cups	rosé	625 mL
1	whole, fresh coho salmon (4 to 5 lb/2 to 2.2 kg)	1
2	lemons, cut in wedges	2
	Hollandaise Sauce (p. 113)	

In saucepan, combine water, shallots, celery, carrot, four sprigs of parsley,
and salt. Bring to boil over medium-high heat; reduce heat and simmer,
uncovered, for 20 minutes.

Pour this stock into fish poacher or large roasting pan. Add rosé.

Wash fish inside and out. Place on rack and into pan. If the fish is not
at least half covered by stock, add up to 1 cup (250 mL) extra water and
more wine as necessary.

Bring stock to just under boiling point so that water appears to shiver
rather than bubble. (If you cook fish faster than this, it will tend to fall
apart.)

Poach, covered, for 35 minutes or just until fish flakes easily when
tested with fork.

Carefully lift rack with fish on it from pan; remove any bits of vegetables. Place fish on platter; garnish with lemon wedges and remaining
parsley. Serve with Hollandaise Sauce (recipe p. 113).

Makes 10 servings.

Grilled Salmon Steaks with Mango Strawberry Cilantro Chutney

The tanginess of strawberries and the sweetness of mango are the perfect combination for grilled salmon. Serve this dish with wild rice and ratatouille.

2	mangoes, semi-ripe	2
1 pint	strawberries	500 mL
1	sweet red pepper, seeds removed	1
1	bunch cilantro or coriander	1
½ cup	water or white wine	125 mL
2 tbsp	honey	25 mL
2 tbsp	curry powder	25 mL
1 tbsp	cinnamon	15 mL
2	salmon steaks (each 6 to 8 oz/170 to 250 g)	2
	Olive or vegetable oil as needed	
	Salt and pepper	

This recipe is FREE of the following triggers (marked ✔)

Caffeine ✔
Chocolate ✔
Citrus fruits ✔
Red wine ✔
Aged cheese ✔
MSG & Nitrates ✔
Aspartame ✔
Nuts ✔
Onions & Garlic ✔
Yeast ✔

Peel mangoes and separate fruit from pit. Dice mango into cubes and set aside. Remove stems from strawberries, cut into quarters and set aside. Dice red pepper into cubes and set aside. Coarsely chop cilantro and set aside.

In small saucepan over medium heat, cook red pepper for 1 minute.

Add mango, water or wine, honey, curry powder, and cinnamon. Reduce heat to low and simmer for approximately 10 minutes or until mixture resembles syrup.

Add strawberries and cilantro and simmer 2 minutes more.

Rub salmon steaks with oil, season with salt and pepper to taste, and grill or broil turning over every 3 minutes. Continue cooking until fish is opaque or until desired doneness.

Place salmon on individual plates and place generous helping of mango chutney in middle.

Makes 2 servings.

Nutrients per serving:
Calories: 342
Protein: 34 grams
Fat: 18 grams
Carbohydrate: 11 grams

MAKE AHEAD: **The chutney can be prepared earlier in the day. Store it in the refrigerator and bring it to room temperature prior to serving.**

Salmon Wrapped in Rice Paper in a Yellow Pepper Sauce

Nutrients per serving:
Calories: 319
Protein: 27 grams
Fat: 15 grams
Carbohydrate: 19 grams

The fresh taste of ginger and garlic blends beautifully with salmon. Serve this exotic dish with a fresh green salad. The commercially made sauces may contain MSG, so read the labels carefully.

4	pieces rice paper	4
1 lb	salmon fillets	500 g
4	sprigs each basil and coriander	4

Marinade

2	cloves garlic, finely chopped	2
1 tbsp	chopped coriander	15 mL
2 tsp	fresh ginger, chopped	10 mL
2 tsp	tamari sauce	10 mL
1 tsp	each oyster sauce, mirin (optional), and sesame oil	5 mL

Sauce

1	clove garlic	1
1	large shallot, finely chopped	1
2	large yellow peppers, cut into small pieces	2
1-½ cups	fish or vegetable stock	375 mL
1 tsp	Extra virgin olive oil	5 mL
	Salt and pepper	

MARINADE:

In bowl, mix together all ingredients.

Pour over salmon fillets and marinate for about 1 hour before assembling dish.

SAUCE:

In saucepan, over medium heat, sauté garlic and shallot. Add yellow peppers; deglaze with stock.

Cover and simmer for 20 minutes or until peppers are tender.

In blender, food processor, or using food mill, process mixture until smooth. Add oil, if necessary.

Season with salt and pepper to taste. Set aside. Sauce should be reheated prior to serving.

TO ASSEMBLE:

Remove fish from marinade. Dry gently removing excess ingredients. Season with salt and pepper to taste.

Dip each piece of rice paper in water until workable. Wrap each salmon fillet in rice paper with sprigs of basil and coriander. In bamboo steamer set above pot of rapidly boiling water, or in fish steamer, steam fillets for 3 to 4 minutes.

Pour reheated yellow pepper sauce on individual plates. Place salmon on top of sauce.

Makes 4 servings.

Pan-Seared River Trout with Cucumber and Baby Shrimp Salsa

Nutrients per serving:
Calories: 361
Protein: 42 grams
Fat: 17 grams
Carbohydrate: 10 grams

The fresh ingredients are what makes this dish so spectacular. Serve it with rice, potatoes, or noodles and your favorite vegetable.

4	river or salmon trout (deboned and dressed)	4
Salsa		
1 cup	baby shrimp	250 mL
1	red onion, diced	1
½	mango, sliced	½
½	sweet red pepper, diced	½
1	English cucumber, ½ diced, ½ sliced	1
2 tbsp	rice wine vinegar	25 mL
2 tbsp	olive oil	25 mL
1 tbsp	chopped fresh dill	15 mL
	Additional oil for sautéing trout	
	Salt and pepper	

Salsa: In bowl, combine shrimp, onion, mango, red pepper, diced cucumber, rice vinegar, olive oil, and dill. (Keep sliced cucumber for garnish.) Mix well and chill.

Over medium heat, heat enough olive oil to generously cover bottom of a 12-inch (30 cm) skillet. Season trout with salt and pepper inside and out. Sauté each trout until golden, about 4 to 5 minutes per side.

Transfer trout to warm plate and decorate with cucumber slices. Top with salsa and serve hot.

Makes 4 servings.

MAKE AHEAD: **Prepare the salsa earlier in the day and refrigerate.**

Baked Halibut with Dill Crust and Red Pepper Sauce

Sometimes it is the simplest ingredients that bring out the best in fish. Fresh dill, red pepper, garlic, and olive oil help to create a uniquely flavorful dish.

Halibut Fillets

½ lb	halibut fillets	250 g
1 tsp	olive oil	5 mL
2 tsp	chopped fresh dill	10 mL
	Salt and pepper	

Place fillets on single piece of aluminum foil; drizzle with olive oil. Top with fresh dill and salt and pepper to taste.

Wrap fillets tightly in foil and place on baking sheet. Bake in 375°F (190°C) oven for 10 to 12 minutes or until fish flakes easily when tested with fork.

Serve with Red Pepper Sauce (recipe follows).

Red Pepper Sauce

1	red pepper, cored and seeded	1
1	clove garlic, chopped	1
1 tbsp	olive oil	15 mL
	Salt and pepper	

Cut pepper into large pieces. In bowl, toss pepper pieces with garlic and oil.

Roast in oven until well colored.

In food processor, process until smooth. Pass through sieve; season with salt and pepper to taste.

Makes 2 servings.

This recipe is FREE of the following triggers (marked ✔)

Caffeine	✔
Chocolate	✔
Citrus fruits	✔
Red wine	✔
Aged cheese	✔
MSG & Nitrates	✔
Aspartame	✔
Nuts	✔
Onions & Garlic	
Yeast	✔

Nutrients per serving:
Calories: 224
Protein: 26 grams
Fat: 12 grams
Carbohydrate: 3 grams

Lemon Sole with Oranges and Honey

Nutrients per serving:
Calories: 505
Protein: 40 grams
Fat: 13 grams
Carbohydrate: 57 grams

In this wonderful recipe, the delicate flavor of lemon sole is paired with the tanginess of oranges and the sublime sweetness of honey.

1 cup	wild rice	250 mL
2 tbsp	butter	25 mL
4	shallots, finely chopped	4
1 cup	dry white wine	250 mL
1 cup	orange juice	250 mL
2 tsp	grated orange rind	10 mL
	Salt and pepper	
	Clear honey	
8	lemon sole fillets	8
2 tbsp	all-purpose flour	25 mL
	Oil for shallow frying	
2	oranges, peeled and cut into segments, membranes removed	2
2 tbsp	chopped fresh parsley	25 mL

In large saucepan of boiling salted water, cook wild rice for 40 to 45 minutes or according to package instructions or until tender.

In large saucepan, melt butter and add shallots; cook for 3 minutes.

Add wine, orange juice, and orange rind. Bring to boil and continue boiling until reduced by half. Season with salt and pepper to taste. Add honey to taste. Cover and keep warm.

Coat sole with flour and season well. In frying pan, heat oil; add fish in batches and cook for 3 minutes on each side or until fish is opaque. Keep warm.

Drain rice. Stir in orange segments. Spoon onto warmed serving dish and place fish on top. Pour sauce over fish and garnish with parsley.

Makes 4 servings.

Scallops with White Wine and Tarragon Sauce

Enjoy tender scallops in a creamy herb and wine sauce—without the cream! Serve with rice or pasta.

1 lb	large sea scallops (about 16)	500 g
2 tbsp	margarine, divided	30 mL
½ cup	diced shallots	125 mL
½ cup	diced carrots	125 mL
2 tbsp	minced sweet red pepper	25 mL
1	clove garlic, minced	1
2 tbsp	all-purpose flour	25 mL
½ cup	dry white wine	125 mL
1 cup	2% milk	250 mL
2 tbsp	chopped fresh parsley	25 mL
1 tbsp	chopped fresh tarragon	15 mL
	Salt and pepper	
2 tbsp	chopped chives	25 mL

This recipe is FREE of the following triggers (marked ✔)

Caffeine	✔
Chocolate	✔
Citrus fruits	✔
Red wine	✔
Aged cheese	✔
MSG & Nitrates	✔
Aspartame	✔
Nuts	✔
Onions & Garlic	
Yeast	✔

Nutrients per serving:
Calories: 215
Protein: 23 grams
Fat: 7 grams
Carbohydrate: 15 grams

Rinse scallops under cold water and dry with paper towel.

In large skillet over medium heat, melt 1 tbsp (15 mL) margarine. Cook scallops for 1 minute per side. Remove and set aside.

Melt remaining margarine. Add shallots, carrots, and pepper; sauté for 5 minutes. Stir in garlic; sauté for 1 minute. Stir in flour; cook for 1 minute. Pour in wine, stirring constantly.

Gradually stir in milk, stirring constantly, until sauce comes to boil. Reduce heat and simmer, stirring occasionally, for 3 minutes.

Stir in scallops, parsley, and tarragon. Cook for 30 seconds. Season to taste with salt and pepper. Pour into serving dish or spoon onto plates and garnish with chopped chives.

Makes 4 servings.

VARIATION:
Substitute fresh dill for tarragon.

Grilled Shrimp with Two Marinades

Nutrients per serving:
Calories: 45
Protein: 7 grams
Fat: 1 gram
Carbohydrate: 2 grams

If you enjoy the delicate flavors of orange and sesame, then you'll love the orange-sesame marinade. However, if you're in the mood for something a little more assertive, the zestiness of balsamic vinegar might be just the thing.

| 20 | medium or large shrimp, shelled and deveined with tails intact | 20 |

Orange-Sesame Marinade

3 tbsp	orange juice concentrate	50 mL
1 tsp	sesame oil	5 mL
	Pepper	

Balsamic Vinegar and Garlic Marinade

2 tbsp	olive oil	25 mL
1-½ tsp	balsamic vinegar	7 mL
½ tsp	Worcestershire sauce	2 mL
1	clove garlic, minced	1
	Cayenne pepper	

In glass bowl, mix ingredients for marinade of choice.

Add shrimp and toss to coat. Marinate for 1 hour at room temperature.

Grill over medium heat, turning frequently, for about 5 minutes or until shrimp are bright pink. Do not overcook.

Makes 4 servings.

Shrimp and Carrot Risotto

Here's a risotto recipe that combines the earthiness of Arborio rice with tender morsels of shrimp and cooked carrot for a dash of color.

3	carrots, peeled and chopped	3
2 tbsp	olive oil	25 mL
3	shallots, peeled and sliced	3
1-½ cups	Arborio rice	375 mL
½ cup	carrot cooking liquid (reserved from Step #2)	125 mL
3 cups	vegetable stock (see p. 110)	750 mL
1 cup	carrot, peeled and grated	1
3 tbsp	unsalted butter	50 mL
16	medium shrimp, peeled, deveined, and precooked	16
	Salt and pepper	
	Fresh Italian parsley, chopped	

This recipe is FREE of the following triggers (marked ✔)

Caffeine ✔
Chocolate ✔
Citrus fruits ✔
Red wine ✔
Aged cheese ✔
MSG & Nitrates ✔
Aspartame ✔
Nuts ✔
Onions & Garlic
Yeast ✔

In large saucepan, cover carrots with water. Add pinch salt. Bring to boil; reduce heat and simmer for about 20 minutes or until tender.

Strain carrots and reserve ½ cup (125 mL) cooking liquid for later. In food processor, puree cooked carrots until smooth. Place in bowl and set aside.

In large saucepan, heat olive oil over medium-high heat. Add shallots and cook for about 3 minutes.

Add rice and continue to cook for another 3 minutes. Add carrot cooking liquid and simmer, stirring occasionally, until liquid has been absorbed.

Add 1-½ cups (375 mL) of the vegetable stock, stirring occasionally, until liquid has been absorbed.

Stir in carrot puree, grated carrot, and remaining vegetable stock. Simmer, stirring, until liquid is absorbed and risotto has creamy texture. Add butter and shrimp; stir until butter is incorporated and shrimp are heated through. Serve on individual dinner plates or on large serving platter. Garnish with chopped Italian parsley.

Makes 4 servings.

Nutrients per serving:
Calories: 532
Protein: 14 grams
Fat: 16 grams
Carbohydrate: 83 grams

Portuguese Seafood Risotto

Nutrients per serving
(when recipe serves 6):
Calories: 662
Protein: 41 grams
Fat: 38 grams
Carbohydrate: 39 grams

A delectable combination of fresh shellfish and firm white fish, this creamy rice dish is best served with generous slices of fresh crusty bread.

½ cup	olive oil	125 mL
1	onion, finely chopped	1
3	cloves garlic, finely chopped	3
18	large mussels, scrubbed and bearded	18
12	medium shrimp, shelled and deveined	12
6	medium to large clams, scrubbed	6
¾ lb	salmon fillet	375 g
¾ lb	monkfish, cubed	375 g
2	squid, cleaned and cut into rings	2
1-¼ cup	Arborio rice	300 mL
1 cup	white wine (optional)	250 mL
2 cups	fish stock (see p. 112) or water	500 mL
Pinch	saffron	Pinch
	Salt and pepper	
⅓ cup	butter	75 mL
1 tbsp	chopped coriander	15 mL
1 tbsp	lemon juice	15 mL

In large deep sauté pan or casserole, heat olive oil over medium-high heat. Add onion, garlic, and all shellfish and fish; cook for 2 to 3 minutes. Remove and set aside all shellfish and fish. Discard any clams and mussels that do not open.

To mixture remaining in pan, add rice, stirring, for 2 minutes. Do not allow rice to brown. Add wine, if using, and allow to evaporate over high heat.

Reduce heat to medium. Add fish stock (or water) in small amounts, adding more as liquid is absorbed. Add saffron, and salt and pepper to taste. Stir constantly until rice has creamy texture and is tender but firm, approximately 12 to 15 minutes. Add additional liquid, if necessary.

Add shellfish and fish to risotto and cook for 3 minutes or until heated through. Gently stir in butter, coriander, and lemon juice. Adjust seasoning, if necessary.

Makes 4 to 6 servings.

KITCHEN POINTER: Clams and mussels should be removed as soon as they unclench their shells, otherwise they will become tough. Some shells will open up sooner than others, and the mussels will open up before the clams. Clam and mussel shells that *do not* open should be discarded.

Vegetables and Side Dishes
Stir-Fried Peppers and Sprouts

This recipe is FREE of the following triggers (marked ✔)
Caffeine ✔
Chocolate ✔
Citrus fruits ✔
Red wine ✔
Aged cheese ✔
MSG & Nitrates ✔
Aspartame ✔
Nuts ✔
Onions & Garlic
Yeast ✔

Nutrients per serving:
Calories: 156
Protein: 4 grams
Fat: 12 grams
Carbohydrate: 8 grams

This simple and colorful side dish features bright red and green peppers fried with the tanginess of fresh ginger and bean sprouts.

2 tbsp	cooking oil	25 mL
1 tsp	minced ginger root	5 mL
½ tsp	salt	2 mL
1	green pepper, cut in strips	1
1	red pepper, cut in strips	1
¾ lb	fresh bean sprouts	375 g
¼ cup	chicken stock (see p. 111)	50 mL

In wok or skillet, heat oil. Add ginger, salt, and peppers. Stir-fry for 2 minutes. Add bean sprouts and stir-fry for 1 minute. Add stock; cover, and cook for 2 to 3 minutes or until vegetables are tender.

Makes 2 servings.

Roasted Vegetable Medley

Roasted in their own juices, these vegetables are tender and very flavorful.

6	small red potatoes, peeled if desired, and quartered	6
4	large carrots, peeled if desired, and cut into 3-inch (8 cm) lengths	4
2	small yellow onions, peeled and quartered	2
2	small zucchini, cut into ½-inch (1 cm) slices	2
2 tbsp	olive oil	25 mL
1 tsp	thyme	5 mL
	Salt and pepper	

This recipe is FREE of the following triggers (marked ✔)

Caffeine ✔
Chocolate ✔
Citrus fruits ✔
Red wine ✔
Aged cheese ✔
MSG & Nitrates ✔
Aspartame ✔
Nuts ✔
Onions & Garlic
Yeast ✔

Preheat oven to 425°F (220°C). In bowl, combine potatoes, carrots, and onions and toss with 1-½ tbsp (20 mL) of olive oil. In a separate bowl, toss zucchini with remaining oil. Place all vegetables (except zucchini) in roasting pan. Sprinkle with thyme, and salt and pepper to taste. Roast for about 40 minutes; add zucchini and gently turn vegetables. Return pan to oven and roast for another 15 to 20 minutes or until vegetables are tender.

Makes about 4 servings.

Nutrients per serving:
Calories: 218
Protein: 5 grams
Fat: 6 grams
Carbohydrate: 36 grams

VARIATIONS: Parsnips, turnips, fennel, chunks of celery root, or winter squash also make good vegetables for roasting. Garlic and herbs such as bay leaves can be added for additional flavor.

Asparagus Spears with Apple, Egg, and Poppy Seed Dressing

Nutrients per serving:
Calories: 131
Protein: 6 grams
Fat: 3 grams
Carbohydrate: 20 grams

This dish is best made in late spring or early summer when asparagus is at its peak. A perfect accompaniment to grilled meats, it also works well as part of an antipasto plate. Make sure you have hard boiled eggs on hand for this recipe.

24	spears fresh asparagus	24
2 to 3	hard boiled eggs	2 to 3
1 cup	apple juice	250 mL
½ cup	apple cider vinegar	125 mL
2 tbsp	honey	25 mL
1 tbsp	poppy seeds	15 mL
	Salt and pepper	

Wash asparagus; snap off tough ends and peel remaining stems. In large skillet of boiling water, blanch asparagus for about 15 to 20 seconds or until barely tender. Immediately immerse cooked asparagus in ice water to stop cooking process. Set aside.

Peel eggs and separate yolks from whites. Grate yolks into bowl. Add apple juice, apple cider vinegar, honey, and poppy seeds; whisk using only as much cider vinegar as required to make pourable sauce.

Dice egg white. Reheat asparagus in hot water; drain and place six spears per guest on individual salad plates. Pour sauce over asparagus and decorate with diced egg whites.

Makes 4 servings.

Charred Zucchini with Herbs, Garlic, and Ricotta

Salting and draining the zucchini prevents excess liquid from watering down this light and tasty side dish.

2	medium green or yellow zucchini	2
	Salt	
1 tsp	olive oil	5 mL
2	stems fresh thyme	2
Pinch	dried oregano	Pinch
1 tbsp	fresh chopped basil (and/or Italian parsley)	15 mL
2	cloves garlic, minced	2
½ cup	fresh ricotta cheese or goat cheese	125 mL
1 tsp	dry breadcrumbs	5 mL
1 tsp	melted butter	5 mL

This recipe is FREE of the following triggers (marked ✔)
Caffeine ✔
Chocolate ✔
Citrus fruits ✔
Red wine ✔
Aged cheese ✔
MSG & Nitrates ✔
Aspartame ✔
Nuts ✔
Onions & Garlic
Yeast

Cut zucchini in half lengthwise. Sprinkle with salt and let sit for about 20 minutes. Dry zucchini with paper towel and coat with olive oil.

Grill or broil zucchini halves on high heat for about 3 minutes. Toss immediately with herbs and garlic. Let cool slightly; slice. In ovenproof dish, toss with ricotta and top with breadcrumbs and butter. Place under broiler to melt cheese. Serve immediately.

Makes 4 servings.

Nutrients per serving:
Calories: 89
Protein: 5 grams
Fat: 5 grams
Carbohydrate: 6 grams

KITCHEN POINTER: **Make sure not to overcook the zucchini or the whole dish will become soggy.**

Roasted New Potatoes with Herbs

Nutrients per serving:
Calories: 248
Protein: 4 grams
Fat: 12 grams
Carbohydrate: 31 grams

In this side dish, new red potatoes are perfectly offset by a delicate combination of garlic, rosemary, and thyme. Serve with roasted chicken, turkey, or pork.

3 lbs	new red potatoes, quartered	1.5 kg
6 tbsp	olive oil (or canola oil)	100 mL
3	cloves garlic, minced	3
1 tbsp	each dried rosemary and thyme	15 mL
1 tsp	dried oregano	5 mL
	Salt and pepper	

In large bowl, combine potatoes, oil, and garlic; toss to coat. Add herbs and toss again. Season with salt and pepper to taste. Divide potatoes between 2 large heavy baking sheets. Bake in 500°F (260°C) oven for about 30 minutes or until brown and crisp, stirring occasionally.

Makes 8 servings.

Mushrooms and Rice

The earthy texture of rice is a perfect match with fresh mushrooms. Serve this quick-cooking side dish with your favorite grilled meats.

¼ cup	butter	50 mL
½ cup	finely chopped onion	125 mL
¼ cup	finely chopped celery	50 mL
3 cups	sliced mushrooms	750 mL
½ tsp	dried thyme and sage	2 mL
	Cooked rice (enough for six servings)	
	Fresh parsley, chopped	
	Salt and pepper	

In large skillet, melt butter over medium heat; cook onion and celery until soft. Add mushrooms, thyme, and sage. Cook, stirring for 3 to 4 minutes. Add mixture to cooked rice; stir in parsley. Salt and pepper to taste.

Makes 6 servings.

This recipe is FREE of the following triggers (marked ✔)

Caffeine ✔
Chocolate ✔
Citrus fruits ✔
Red wine ✔
Aged cheese ✔
MSG & Nitrates ✔
Aspartame ✔
Nuts ✔
Onions & Garlic
Yeast ✔

Nutrients per serving:
Calories: 171
Protein: 3 grams
Fat: 7 grams
Carbohydrate: 24 grams

Steamed Basmati Rice with Crisp Potatoes, Sumac, and Cumin

Nutrients per serving (when recipe serves 8):
Calories: 341
Protein: 5 grams
Fat: 9 grams
Carbohydrate: 60 grams

Fragrant basmati tops a layer of crispy sweet potatoes in this Middle Eastern-inspired side dish.

1 lb	basmati rice	500 g
1/3 cup	olive oil	75 mL
3	sweet potatoes, peeled and sliced 1/4 inch (5 mm) thick	3
1	lemon zest, cut in julienne only	1
1 tbsp	each ground cumin and sumac	15 mL
	Salt and pepper	

In large saucepan of boiling water, cook rice for about 10 minutes or until 50 percent cooked. Strain off water and set aside.

Place 2 tbsp (25 mL) olive oil in stainless steel pot with lid. Arrange sweet potato slices side by side to cover entire bottom of pot. Begin scooping rice into center of pot to form dome shape. Once all rice is in, lightly pat down, maintaining shape within 1/4-inch (5 mm) diameter of edges. Probe breather holes in rice, penetrating down to bottom. Lightly drizzle rice with remaining olive oil and season with lemon zest, cumin, sumac, and salt and pepper to taste.

Place damp dish towel over pot, place lid on, fold remaining towel over lid and place pot on stove top. Cook over medium-high heat for about 7 minutes or until potatoes are crispy.

Serve immediately.

Makes 6 to 8 servings.

Wild Cherry Tabbouleh

The nuttiness of bulgur is perfectly offset by the sweetness of cherries in this dish. Serve with your favorite grilled meats or as a main course salad with some bread. This salad makes an excellent addition to any picnic basket because it should be served at room temperature.

1 cup	bulgur (available at health food or bulk stores)	250 mL
2 cups	boiling water or chicken stock (see p. 111)	500 mL
2 cups	fresh cherries, pitted and split	500 mL
2 tbsp	each chopped fresh mint and parsley	25 mL
	Salt and pepper	
	Sunflower oil, as needed	

In medium bowl, gradually add boiling water or chicken stock to bulgur until bulgur has absorbed enough water to allow it to swell and become tender, but not soggy.

Add cherries, mint, parsley, and salt and pepper to taste and mix thoroughly. Allow to stand for approximately 30 minutes in cool place.

Check seasoning and adjust, adding more water or stock and sunflower oil, if necessary.

Makes 4 to 6 servings.

KITCHEN POINTER: **Cherry pitters are available at kitchen supply stores. This gadget makes pitting cherries easier than having to cut the cherries in half and then prying out the pit.**

MAKE AHEAD: **The tabbouleh can be prepared earlier in the day or a day in advance. Store in the refrigerator and bring to room temperature before serving.**

This recipe is FREE of the following triggers (marked ✔)

Caffeine ✔
Chocolate ✔
Citrus fruits ✔
Red wine ✔
Aged cheese ✔
MSG & Nitrates ✔
Aspartame ✔
Nuts ✔
Onions & Garlic ✔
Yeast ✔

Nutrients per serving
(when recipe serves 6):
Calories: 109
Protein: 3 grams
Fat: 1 gram
Carbohydrate: 22 grams

Bulgur and Green Bean Salad with Herbed Vinaigrette

Bulgur is parboiled cracked wheat that is easy to prepare and has a nutty flavor and pleasant chewy texture.

2 cups	bulgur	500 mL
2 cups	boiling water	500 mL
¾ lb	green beans	375 mL
⅓ cup	balsamic vinegar (or cider vinegar and 1 tsp/5 mL brown sugar)	75 mL
3	cloves garlic, minced	3
1 tsp	each chopped fresh thyme, oregano, and rosemary	5 mL
1 cup	olive oil (or canola oil)	250 mL
	Salt and pepper	
3	medium tomatoes, chopped	3
1 cup	chopped, pitted kalamata olives	250 mL
4 cups	mixed greens (mesclun)	1 L
½ lb	soft mild goat cheese, crumbled	250 g

Nutrients per serving
(when recipe serves 8):
Calories: 336
Protein: 12 grams
Fat: 16 grams
Carbohydrate: 36 grams

KITCHEN POINTER: **Chicken can be added to this dish to make a complete meal.**

In large bowl, combine bulgur and water. Set aside.

In saucepan, cook green beans in boiling salted water for about 4 minutes or until tender but crisp. Drain well. Pat dry. Add to bulgur.

In medium bowl, combine vinegar, garlic, and herbs. Gradually whisk in oil. Season to taste with salt and pepper.

Add tomatoes and olives to bulgur. Mix in enough vinaigrette to coat completely. Season with salt and pepper to taste.

Mound mixed greens on platter. Top with bulgur; add crumbled goat cheese as garnish.

Makes 6 to 8 servings.

Grilled Polenta with Tomato Sauce

In this recipe, the polenta is allowed to harden and then it's sliced, grilled, and served with tomato sauce to make a zesty side dish.

2	shallots, diced	2
2 tbsp	vegetable oil or butter	25 mL
½ cup	fresh corn, whole kernels	125 mL
1	red pepper, diced	1
1 tsp	finely chopped garlic	5 mL
4 cups	milk	1 L
4 cups	chicken stock (see p. 111)	1 L
2 cups	fine cornmeal	500 mL
1 tbsp	each chopped fresh mixed herbs (rosemary, thyme, *etc.*)	15 mL
½	lemon, juiced	½
	Salt and pepper	
¾ cup	tomato sauce	175 mL

This recipe is FREE of the following triggers (marked ✔)
Caffeine ✔
Chocolate ✔
Citrus fruits
Red wine ✔
Aged cheese ✔
MSG & Nitrates ✔
Aspartame ✔
Nuts ✔
Onions & Garlic
Yeast ✔

Nutrients per serving (when recipe serves 6):
Calories: 353
Protein: 12 grams
Fat: 9 grams
Carbohydrate: 56 grams

In large saucepan, heat oil and cook shallots until tender. Add corn, red pepper, and garlic; cook until tender.

Add milk and chicken stock; bring to boil over medium heat. Slowly whisk in cornmeal. Add herbs, lemon juice, and salt and pepper to taste. Cook for additional 5 to 10 minutes or until creamy and thick.

Pour polenta into 9-inch (2.5 L) square cake pan, lined with plastic wrap. Gently tap pan to ensure polenta gets into all corners. Allow to cool. Cover and refrigerate for 2 hours (or overnight).

To serve, unmold polenta and remove plastic wrap. Slice into ¼- or ½-inch (5 mm or 1 cm) pieces and cut on diagonal to form two triangles. On preheated grill, grill polenta until heated through, turning once.

Meanwhile, in saucepan over medium-low heat, heat tomato sauce. Spoon some tomato sauce onto individual plates. Arrange two triangles per person on top. Garnish with sprig of fresh rosemary or thyme.

Makes 4 to 6 servings.

KITCHEN POINTER: If fresh corn is unavailable, frozen or canned whole kernels can be substituted.

MAKE AHEAD: Prepare polenta and refrigerate up to a day in advance. Then grill.

Basic Stocks and Sauces

Vegetable Stock

Here's a flavorful meatless stock that will keep in the refrigerator for one week or can be frozen for later use.

1 tbsp	olive oil	15 mL
3 cups	sliced carrots	750 mL
3 cups	sliced onions	750 mL
2 cups	chopped savoy cabbage	500 mL
2 cups	sliced leeks	500 mL
1-½ cups	sliced celery	375 mL
1 cup	peeled and sliced parsnips	250 mL
½ cup	parsley sprigs	125 mL
3	cloves garlic	3
2	fresh thyme sprigs	2
2 tbsp	chopped fresh basil	25 mL
1	bay leaf	1
1 tsp	whole black peppercorns	5 mL
2 tsp	kosher sea salt	10 mL
1	medium potato, sliced	1
2	medium tomatoes, chopped	2
12 cups	water	3 L

In stockpot over medium-high heat, heat olive oil. Add remaining ingredients except potato, tomatoes, and water. Cook, stirring occasionally, for about 6 to 8 minutes or until vegetables soften.

Add potato, tomatoes, and water. Bring to boil; lower heat and simmer, covered, for 40 minutes. Strain stock through colander over bowl, pressing down on vegetables to extract as much stock as possible.

Refrigerate to cool. Once stock is cold, it should be tightly covered.

Makes about 12 cups (3 L) stock.

Chicken or Beef Stock

Canned soups and powdered stock mixes often contain MSG or other preservatives that can be triggers. Fortunately, a flavorful chicken or beef stock is not difficult to make, and if onions and garlic are triggers for you, they can be omitted from the recipe.

	Beef or chicken bones to fill 8-quart (8 L) pot (brown beef bones first for richer broth)	
2 cups	chopped celery	500 mL
2	medium carrots, chopped	2
2	medium onions, chopped	2
½ tsp	each oregano and thyme	2 mL
2 tsp	chopped fresh parsley	10 mL
2	bay leaves	2
2	cloves garlic	2
1 tbsp	salt	15 mL
8	peppercorns	8
4	whole cloves	4

This recipe is FREE of the following triggers (marked ✔)

Caffeine ✔
Chocolate ✔
Citrus fruits ✔
Red wine ✔
Aged cheese ✔
MSG & Nitrates ✔
Aspartame ✔
Nuts ✔
Onions & Garlic
Yeast ✔

Place bones in stockpot over medium-high heat. Add all remaining ingredients and cover with water. (If omitting onions and garlic, add extra bay leaf and another carrot or parsnip). Bring to boil; lower heat and simmer covered for 4 to 6 hours. Strain in colander over large bowl. Discard bones and vegetables. Refrigerate stock overnight; remove fat.

Nutrients:
Contains less than 10 calories per 1 cup (250 mL) and trace amounts of protein, fat, and carbohydrates.

Makes 12 to 16 cups (3 to 4 L) stock.

KITCHEN POINTER: **This stock can be stored in batches in the freezer and used as the base for many homemade soups.**

Fish Stock

This versatile stock can be refrigerated for up to five days or frozen for up to six months.

12 cups	water	3 L
1 cup	dry white wine	250 mL
4 lb	fish trimmings, washed	2 kg
2	celery sticks, sliced	2
1	onion, sliced	1
2 tbsp	lemon juice	25 mL
6	peppercorns	6
4	fresh parsley sprigs	4
2	fresh thyme sprigs or ½ tsp (2 mL) dried	2

Nutrients:

Contains less than 10 calories per 1 cup (250 mL) and trace amounts of protein, fat, and carbohydrates.

In stockpot, bring water and wine to boil over high heat. Add fish trimmings, celery, and onion.

Add all remaining ingredients. When water returns to boil, reduce heat so that stock is barely simmering; simmer for 2-½ to 3 hours.

Strain stock, extracting as much liquid as possible from solids. Discard solids and allow stock to reach room temperature before refrigerating or freezing.

Makes about 12 cups (3 L) stock.

Hollandaise Sauce

Serve this sauce over poached salmon (see p. 88), Eggs Benedict, or asparagus.

6	egg yolks	6
2 tbsp	lemon juice	25 mL
½ lb	butter, melted	250 g
¼ cup	hot water	50 mL
Pinch	cayenne pepper	Pinch
	Salt	

In top of double boiler or in metal bowl placed over saucepan of hot, but not simmering, water, beat egg yolks with wire whisk until smooth.

Add lemon juice and gradually whisk in melted butter, pouring in thin stream.

Slowly stir in hot water, cayenne pepper, and salt to taste. Continue to mix for about 1 minute or until sauce is thickened.

Serve immediately.

Makes about 2 cups (500 mL).

This recipe is FREE of the following triggers (marked ✔)

Caffeine ✔
Chocolate ✔
Citrus fruits
Red wine ✔
Aged cheese ✔
MSG & Nitrates ✔
Aspartame ✔
Nuts ✔
Onions & Garlic ✔
Yeast ✔

Nutrients per serving (2 tbsp/25 mL serving):
Calories: 103
Protein: 1 gram
Fat: 11 grams
Carbohydrate: trace

Homemade Soy Sauce

This recipe is FREE of the following triggers (marked ✔)
Caffeine ✔
Chocolate ✔
Citrus fruits ✔
Red wine ✔
Aged cheese ✔
MSG & Nitrates ✔
Aspartame ✔
Nuts ✔
Onions & Garlic ✔
Yeast ✔

Nutrients per serving:
1 tbsp/15 mL contains less
than 10 calories and very
small amounts of protein
and carbohydrate.

Most commercially made soy sauce contains MSG, a common trigger for migraine. If you cannot find naturally brewed soy sauce, you might want to consider this recipe for concentrated beef broth. This sauce can be used as a substitute for soy sauce.

¾ cup	beef drippings	175 mL
¼ cup	water	50 mL
	Sea salt, if desired	

Next time you make roast beef, instead of making gravy, save drippings. After drippings are cool, make sure to skim off fat.

In bowl, mix beef drippings with water. Add sea salt, if desired.

Store this sauce in airtight container in the freezer, for up to three months.

Quick Breads

Never-Fail Biscuits

These fluffy white biscuits are an excellent accompaniment to any meal. They can also be served simply with butter and jam.

2 cups	all-purpose flour	500 mL
4 tsp	baking powder	20 mL
1 tsp	granulated sugar	5 mL
½ tsp	salt	2 mL
½ cup	margarine	125 mL
⅔ cup	milk	150 mL
1	egg	1

This recipe is FREE of the following triggers (marked ✔)

Caffeine ✔
Chocolate ✔
Citrus fruits ✔
Red wine ✔
Aged cheese ✔
MSG & Nitrates ✔
Aspartame ✔
Nuts ✔
Onions & Garlic ✔
Yeast ✔

In large bowl, blend together flour, baking powder, sugar, and salt. Finely cut in margarine. Add milk and egg; mix well. Place dough on lightly floured surface. Roll or pat to desired thickness. Cut with floured round biscuit cutter.

Tranfer rounds to lightly greased baking sheet. Bake in 450°F (230°C) oven for 10 to 12 minutes or until lightly browned.

Makes about 15 biscuits (if using 2-inch/5 cm round cutter).

Nutrients per serving:
Calories: 131
Protein: 3 grams
Fat: 7 grams
Carbohydrate: 14 grams

Healthy Biscuits

Nutrients per serving:
Calories: 181
Protein: 4 grams
Fat: 9 grams
Carbohydrate: 21 grams

Spelt is a type of wheat. The combination of spelt and oat flours produces a surprisingly light biscuit with a rich, nutty flavor. This recipe can be doubled with good results.

1-¼ cups	spelt flour	300 mL
1-¼ cups	oat flour	300 mL
2 tsp	baking powder	10 mL
¼ tsp	baking soda	1 mL
¼ tsp	sea salt	1 mL
½ cup	butter	125 mL
¾ cup	buttermilk	175 mL

In large bowl, combine flours, baking powder, baking soda, and salt; cut in butter until mixture resembles coarse crumbs (using hands usually works best for this). Stir in buttermilk to form soft dough.

Turn out onto lightly floured surface and knead dough gently. Roll out to about ½-inch (1 cm) thickness and cut into 2-½-inch (6 cm) rounds with biscuit cutter (or any size you prefer)—a drinking glass can even be used for this purpose. Transfer to lightly greased baking sheet and bake in 375°F (190°C) oven for about 10 minutes or until just golden on top. (Watch carefully as every oven is different.)

Makes about 12 biscuits.

VARIATIONS: **This biscuit can be baked as a sweet bread (scone) by adding 1 tsp (5 mL) sugar and ¼ cup (50 mL) raisins or chopped candied ginger. For savory biscuits, add chopped fresh herbs or dry herbs.**

Irish Scones

Made with rolled oats and raisins, these scones are a nutritious and tasty alternative to ordinary scones.

2-½ cups	all-purpose flour	625 mL
¼ cup	rolled oats	50 mL
2 tbsp	granulated sugar	25 mL
2 tsp	baking powder	10 mL
2 tsp	baking soda	10 mL
½ tsp	salt	2 mL
⅓ cup	shortening or butter	75 mL
1-¼ cups	milk	300 mL
½ cup	raisins	125 mL

This recipe is FREE of the following triggers (marked ✔)

Caffeine ✔
Chocolate ✔
Citrus fruits ✔
Red wine ✔
Aged cheese ✔
MSG & Nitrates ✔
Aspartame ✔
Nuts ✔
Onions & Garlic ✔
Yeast ✔

Nutrients per serving:
Calories: 194
Protein: 4 grams
Fat: 6 grams
Carbohydrate: 31 grams

Mix together flour, oats, sugar, baking powder, baking soda, and salt. With pastry blender or two knives, cut in shortening or butter. Add milk and stir in raisins.

Turn dough out onto lightly floured surface. Pat or roll out to ¾-inch (2 cm) thickness. Cut into rounds using a 2-inch (5 cm) cutter. Bake in 400°F (200°C) oven for 10 to 15 minutes or until golden brown.

Makes about 12 scones.

KITCHEN POINTER: The secret to light and fluffy biscuits or scones is to work the dough as little as possible. Pastry or baking soda dough toughens the more you work it because the gluten in the flour is activated.

Buttermilk Scones

A healthy alternative to sweet scones, these can also be served as a savory appetizer with your favorite cheese.

3 cups	all-purpose flour	750 mL
1 tbsp	baking powder	15 mL
1-½ tsp	salt	7 mL
1 to 2 cups	buttermilk	250 to 500 mL

In large bowl, sift together flour, baking powder, and salt. Gradually add 1 cup (250 mL) buttermilk. Add enough buttermilk to make stiff dough.

Turn out onto lightly floured board and roll out to about ¾-inch (2 cm) thickness. Cut with large round cookie cutter. Bake in 350°F (180°C) oven on ungreased griddle or on greased baking sheet for about 25 minutes or until golden brown.

Makes about 12 scones.

Nutrients per serving:
Calories: 129
Protein: 4 grams
Fat: 1 gram
Carbohydrate: 26 grams

Corn Bread

Sure to bring back memories of home, this corn bread is wonderful accompanied by a bowl of steaming chili.

2 cups	biscuit mix	500 mL
1 cup	cornmeal	250 mL
¾ cup	granulated sugar	175 mL
½ tsp	baking soda	2 mL
½ tsp	salt	2 mL
1 cup	light cream	250 mL
1 cup	margarine	250 mL
2	eggs, lightly beaten	2

In large bowl, mix biscuit mix, cornmeal, sugar, baking soda, and salt. In saucepan, scald cream with margarine; add to dry ingredients. Mix in eggs.

Pour batter into greased and floured 13- x 9-inch (3.5 L) baking dish or pan, spreading evenly. Bake in 350°F (180°C) oven for 30 minutes or until lightly browned and firm to touch. Let stand for several minutes before cutting.

Makes about 12 to 16 servings.

This recipe is FREE of the following triggers (marked ✔)

Caffeine ✔
Chocolate ✔
Citrus fruits ✔
Red wine ✔
Aged cheese ✔
MSG & Nitrates ✔
Aspartame ✔
Nuts ✔
Onions & Garlic ✔
Yeast ✔

Nutrients per serving:
Calories: 260
Protein: 3 grams
Fat: 16 grams
Carbohydrate: 26 grams

Zucchini Bread

Nutrients per serving (1 slice):
Calories: 135
Protein: 2 grams
Fat: 7 grams
Carbohydrate: 16 grams

Rich, moist, fragrant, and delicious, zucchini bread is more of a treat than a bread. It's perfect for breakfast, as a snack, or for dessert.

3	eggs	3
2-½ cups	grated zucchini	625 mL
1 cup	butter, melted	250 mL
1 cup	granulated sugar	250 mL
3 cups	all-purpose flour	750 mL
2 tsp	ground nutmeg	10 mL
1 tsp	baking soda	5 mL
1 tsp	cinnamon	5 mL
1 tsp	salt	5 mL
¼ tsp	baking powder	1 mL

In large bowl, beat eggs well. Blend in zucchini, butter, and sugar.

In separate bowl, sift flour, nutmeg, baking soda, cinnamon, salt, and baking powder. Stir into zucchini mixture.

Pour batter into 2 greased loaf pans. Bake in 325°F (160°C) oven for 1 hour or until tester inserted in center comes out clean. Let cool in pan for 10 minutes, then turn out onto rack to cool completely.

Makes 2 loaves.

VARIATION: Stir ½ cup (125 mL) raisins into batter before pouring into loaf pans.

Big Loonie Pancakes

Kids love these loonie-sized cakes served with sweetened strawberries or with butter and maple syrup.

2	eggs, separated	2
¾ to 1 cup	milk	175 to 250 mL
1 tbsp	oil	15 mL
1 cup	all-purpose flour	250 mL

In large bowl, beat egg whites until stiff. In blender, blend egg yolks. Add milk to egg yolks and blend. Blend in oil. Add flour and blend. Fold this mixture into beaten egg whites.

Heat nonstick griddle to 400°F (200°C) or heat nonstick skillet or griddle over medium heat. Using less than ¼ cup (50 mL) batter for each pancake, pour onto hot griddle. When underside is brown and bubbles break on topside, turn over and bake until second side is golden.

Makes about 12 pancakes (more if you use less batter per pancake).

This recipe is FREE of the following triggers (marked ✔)

Caffeine ✔
Chocolate ✔
Citrus fruits ✔
Red wine ✔
Aged cheese ✔
MSG & Nitrates ✔
Aspartame ✔
Nuts ✔
Onions & Garlic ✔
Yeast ✔

Nutrients per serving:
Calories: 66
Protein: 3 grams
Fat: 2 grams
Carbohydrate: 9 grams

Apple Pancakes

Nutrients per serving:
Calories: 97
Protein: 3 grams
Fat: 1 gram
Carbohydrate: 19 grams

These tasty pancakes are ideal for a special-day breakfast for two or three people.

1-½ cups	all-purpose flour	375 mL
1 tbsp	granulated sugar	15 mL
1 tbsp	baking powder	15 mL
½ tsp	salt	2 mL
1	egg, beaten	1
1-½ cups	milk	375 mL
2	small apples, finely chopped	2
1 tsp	cinnamon	5 mL

Mix together flour, sugar, baking powder, and salt.

In separate bowl, mix egg and milk; add to dry mixture. Add chopped apples and cinnamon, stirring only until batter is moistened.

Heat nonstick skillet or griddle over medium heat. Pour batter onto griddle using about ¼ cup (50 mL) for each pancake. When underside is brown and bubbles break on topside, turn over and continue cooking until second side is golden brown. Serve with Apple Syrup (recipe follows).

Makes about 12 pancakes.

Apple Syrup

1-½ cups	chopped, peeled apple	375 mL
¾ cup plus 2 tsp	apple juice (divided)	175 mL plus 10 mL
½ cup	maple syrup	125 mL
2 tsp	cornstarch	10 mL

In saucepan, combine apples, ¾ cup (175 mL) apple juice, and maple syrup. Bring to boil over medium heat, stirring occasionally. Reduce heat, cover, and simmer for 10 minutes or until apples are tender.

In small bowl, combine cornstarch and 2 tsp (10 mL) apple juice. Add to hot mixture; cook stirring until slightly thickened. Serve warm over apple pancakes.

Desserts and Baked Goods

Apple Cobbler

This delectable cobbler is made with rolled oats and is quick and easy to prepare. Serve it plain or with whipped cream or vanilla ice cream.

3	Empire apples, peeled and cored	3
½ cup	apple juice	125 mL
¼ cup	granulated sugar	50 mL
1 tbsp	cinnamon	15 mL
1 tsp	nutmeg	5 mL
1 cup	uncooked rolled oats	250 mL
1 cup	brown sugar	250 mL
½ cup	all-purpose flour	125 mL
½ cup	unsalted butter	125 mL

Cut apples into ¼-inch (5 mm) slices.

In small saucepan, combine apples, apple juice, granulated sugar, cinnamon, and nutmeg.

Cook mixture over medium heat for approximately 10 minutes, stirring occasionally, or until mixture becomes syrupy.

In bowl, mix rolled oats, brown sugar, flour, and butter until thoroughly combined and mixture resembles pea-sized shapes.

Pour apple mixture into 4-inch (10 cm) deep baking dish (small loaf pan) and top evenly with oat mixture. Bake in 400°F (200°C) oven for approximately 4 to 5 minutes or until topping is browned and fruit is bubbly.

Makes 2 to 4 servings.

MAKE AHEAD: **The cobbler can be prepared several hours prior to serving and kept at room temperature.**

This recipe is FREE of the following triggers (marked ✔)

Caffeine ✔
Chocolate ✔
Citrus fruits ✔
Red wine ✔
Aged cheese ✔
MSG & Nitrates ✔
Aspartame ✔
Nuts ✔
Onions & Garlic ✔
Yeast ✔

Nutrients per serving (when recipe serves 4):
Calories: 706
Protein: 6 grams
Fat: 26 grams
Carbohydrate: 112 grams

Roasted Pears with Mint Anglaise

Serve this elegant dessert garnished with fresh mint or with a scoop of your favorite ice cream.

1 cup	granulated sugar	250 mL
1 cup	water	250 mL
4	pears, firm but ripe (Bartlett, Bosc)	4

Sauce

8	egg yolks	8
1 cup	granulated sugar	250 mL
2 tsp	cornstarch (optional)	10 mL
4 cups	2% milk	1 L
1	bunch fresh mint, chopped	1
	Extra mint for garnish	

Nutrients per serving (1 pear with ¼ cup/ 50 mL sauce):
Calories: 225
Protein: 4 grams
Fat: 5 grams
Carbohydrate: 41 grams

In heavy saucepan, combine sugar and water. Bring to boil and allow to boil for several minutes only. Remove from heat and allow to cool. This makes a simple syrup.

Peel and core pears. Wrap stems with aluminum foil. Cut pears in curvilinear pattern so that pear will fan out on plate. Dip pears in simple syrup.

Arrange pears on greased baking sheet and cook in 400°F (200°C) oven for about 30 minutes or until caramel in color.

SAUCE:

In stainless steel bowl, whisk together egg yolks and sugar. Beat in cornstarch, if using. Set aside.

In saucepan, combine milk and mint. Heat over medium heat, stirring occasionally. Bring milk up to boiling point, stirring often, but do not boil. Strain milk. Gradually, in thin stream, add milk to egg-sugar mixture while constantly whisking.

In top of double boiler over simmering water or in bowl over saucepan filled with simmering water, cook sauce, stirring constantly, until sauce coats back of spoon. Remove from heat and let cool.

To serve, place some Mint Anglaise on dessert plates. Fan out a warm caramelized pear on each plate. Garnish with fresh mint.

Makes 4 servings.

MAKE AHEAD: The Mint Anglaise may be made up to 2 days in advance and stored in a refrigerator.

Poached Fruit in Light Syrup with Vanilla Ice Cream and Roasted Almonds

Nutrients per serving:
Calories: 380
Protein: 4 grams
Fat: 16 grams
Carbohydrate: 55 grams

Vary the fruit in this recipe to suit the season. This elegant and tasty dessert is sure to impress your guests.

2 cups	granulated sugar	500 mL
4 cups	water	1 L
1	pear, cut into wedges	1
1	peach, cut into wedges	1
1 cup	fresh strawberries, hulled	250 mL
8	scoops good quality vanilla ice cream	8
¼ cup	slivered toasted almonds	50 mL

In medium saucepan, combine sugar and water to make syrup. Bring to boil and boil gently, stirring occasionally, for 5 minutes.

Add pear wedges to syrup for 1 minute. Remove pear wedges. Add peach wedges to syrup for 10 seconds; remove from syrup. Add strawberries to syrup for 10 seconds; remove from syrup.

Continue to boil syrup until it reaches slightly thick consistency.

Meanwhile, in 4 champagne flutes, alternate layers of fruit and ice cream. Top with sprinkling of slivered toasted almonds. Using tablespoon, drizzle some of syrup over almonds. Serve immediately.

Makes 4 servings.

Allspice Roasted Bananas

A simple but tasty dessert; perfect with vanilla ice cream.

8	bananas, small to medium	8
2 cups	firmly packed brown sugar	500 mL
½ cup	unsalted butter, melted	125 mL
5	whole allspice	5

In baking dish, top whole peeled bananas with brown sugar. Drizzle melted butter evenly over bananas and sugar. Scatter allspice over top.

Bake in 425°F (220°C) oven for about 10 minutes or until sugar melts, bubbles, and caramelizes leaving bananas soft.

Serve over vanilla ice cream or yogurt.

Makes 6 to 8 servings.

KITCHEN POINTER: Watch oven carefully because bananas burn quickly if left too long.

This recipe is FREE of the following triggers (marked ✔)

Caffeine ✔
Chocolate ✔
Citrus fruits ✔
Red wine ✔
Aged cheese ✔
MSG & Nitrates ✔
Aspartame ✔
Nuts ✔
Onions & Garlic ✔
Yeast ✔

Nutrients per serving
(when recipe serves 8):
Calories: 441
Protein: 1 gram
Fat: 13 grams
Carbohydrate: 80 grams

Blueberry Maple Pie with Warmed Maple Syrup

Nutrients per serving:
Calories: 480
Protein: 4 grams
Fat: 28 grams
Carbohydrate: 53 grams

Maple syrup adds a delectable touch to this blueberry pie that's perfect with vanilla ice cream.

Crust

½ cup	cold water	125 mL
Pinch	salt	Pinch
1 tbsp	maple syrup	15 mL
1 cup	cold shortening	250 mL
1-½ cups	all-purpose flour	375 mL
1	egg (for egg wash)	1

Filling

5 cups	fresh or frozen blueberries	1.25 L
½ cup	granulated sugar	125 mL
¼ cup	maple syrup	50 mL
2 tbsp	cornstarch	25 mL
¼ tsp	cinnamon	1 mL

CRUST:

In small bowl, dissolve salt in cold water; add maple syrup and combine.

In large mixing bowl or food processor, work shortening into flour until mixture resembles coarse meal with some larger pieces.

Make well in center of mixture. Gradually add cold water mixture, using only as much as required to form dough. Without overhandling, knead dough lightly and form into ball. Wrap in plastic wrap and refrigerate for 30 minutes or overnight.

FILLING:

Cut dough in 2 pieces. On lightly floured surface, roll out 1 piece of dough into round to fit 9-inch (23 cm) pie plate with slight overhang. Roll out second piece for top crust.

Opposite: Wild Cherry Tabbouleh (p. 107)
Overleaf: Zucchini Bread (p. 120)

Line bottom of pie plate with dough and gently press into place. Trim excess pastry to edge of pie plate.

Combine blueberries, sugar, maple syrup, cornstarch, and cinnamon. Spread on top of pastry.

Cover with top crust. Trim sealing edges with egg wash (1 egg, with ½ eggshell of water mixed together).

Make several slits in dough to allow steam to vent. Brush top with egg wash.

Bake in 375°F (190°C) oven until juices bubble and crust is golden.

Serve warm or at room temperature with vanilla ice cream topped with warmed maple syrup.

Makes 8 servings.

MAKE AHEAD: **Prepare pastry crust a day in advance. The pie can be baked earlier in the day and then warmed prior to serving.**

Opposite: Peppermint Cooler (p. 147)
Overleaf: Cranberry Carrot Cake with Cream Cheese Frosting (p. 134)

Peach Tart

Nutrients per serving (when recipe serves 10):
Calories: 243
Protein: 3 grams
Fat: 11 grams
Carbohydrate: 33 grams

Peaches, artfully arranged atop a spongy cake and baked in the oven, make an impressive dessert for entertaining. Try serving this with a dollop of whipped cream.

½ cup	butter	125 mL
¾ cup	granulated sugar (or brown)	175 mL
1 cup	all-purpose flour (or whole wheat)	250 mL
1 tsp	baking powder	5 mL
Pinch	salt	Pinch
2	eggs	2
4	peaches, sliced	4
¼ cup	granulated sugar	50 mL
3 tbsp	lemon juice	50 mL
Pinch	each cinnamon and nutmeg	Pinch

In large mixing bowl, cream butter and sugar. Add flour, baking powder, and salt. Add eggs and beat well.

Spread batter in greased 9-inch (2.5 L) springform pan. Place peaches, skin side up, in pattern on top.

Sprinkle with sugar and lemon juice, cinnamon, and nutmeg.

Bake in 350°F (180°C) oven for 1 hour or until peaches are tender and cake is golden.

Makes 8 to 10 servings.

Old-Fashioned Butterscotch Pie

No one can resist the rich buttery goodness of this familiar dessert!

¾ cup	brown sugar	175 mL
2 tbsp	all-purpose flour	25 mL
1-¾ cups	milk (half evaporated)	425 mL
1 tbsp	(approx.) butter	15 mL
2	egg yolks, well beaten	2
1 tsp	vanilla	5 mL
1	baked 9-inch (23 cm) pie shell	1

In bowl, mix brown sugar and flour. Stir in milk.

In saucepan, cook mixture over medium heat until thick.

Remove from heat. Add butter and egg yolks. Return to heat and cook 2 minutes longer. Remove from heat.

Stir in vanilla; pour mixture into pre-baked pie shell and spread evenly. Top with meringue (recipe follows).

Meringue for Butterscotch Pie

2	egg whites	2
¼ cup	granulated sugar	50 mL

In bowl, beat egg whites until soft peaks form. Very gradually beat in sugar until mixture is stiff. Spread evenly over filling. Bake in 425°F (220°C) oven for 4 to 5 minutes or until tips of meringue are golden. Remove from oven and let cool. Chill before serving.

Makes 8 servings.

This recipe is FREE of the following triggers (marked ✔)

Caffeine ✔
Chocolate ✔
Citrus fruits ✔
Red wine ✔
Aged cheese ✔
MSG & Nitrates ✔
Aspartame ✔
Nuts ✔
Onions & Garlic ✔
Yeast ✔

Nutrients per serving:
Calories: 288
Protein: 6 grams
Fat: 12 grams
Carbohydrate: 39 grams

Ginger Pound Cake

**Nutrients per serving
(when recipe serves 12):**
Calories: 426
Protein: 5 grams
Fat: 18 grams
Carbohydrate: 61 grams

Ginger adds a unique taste to this simple and delicious cake.

1 cup	butter	250 mL
1-½ cups	fruit sugar	375 mL
4	eggs	4
1 tsp	vanilla	5 mL
2 cups	all-purpose flour	500 mL
½ tsp	baking powder	2 mL
¼ tsp	salt	1 mL
1 cup	ginger marmalade	250 mL

In large bowl, cream butter with sugar until light and fluffy. Add eggs one at a time, beating well after each. Beat in vanilla.

In separate bowl, combine flour, baking powder, and salt. Blend flour mixture into butter mixture. Stir in marmalade.

Turn batter into greased and floured 9- x 5-inch (2 L) or 8- x 4-inch (1.5 L) loaf pan. Bake in 325°F (160°C) oven for about 1-¼ to 1-½ hours or until tester comes out clean. Let cool in pan, then turn out onto rack to cool completely.

Make 8 to 12 servings.

Maple Syrup Cake

Toasted coconut adds a delightful crunchiness to this moist maple cake.

Sauce

1 cup	maple syrup	250 mL
¾ cup	water	175 mL
2 tsp	butter	10 mL

Cake

1 cup	all-purpose flour	250 mL
½ cup	granulated sugar	125 mL
1-½ tsp	baking powder	7 mL
½ tsp	salt	2 mL
1	egg, well beaten	1
⅓ cup	milk	75 mL
1 tbsp	shortening	15 mL
½ cup	shredded coconut	125 mL
	Whipped cream	

This recipe is FREE of the following triggers (marked ✔)

Caffeine ✔
Chocolate ✔
Citrus fruits ✔
Red wine ✔
Aged cheese ✔
MSG & Nitrates ✔
Aspartame ✔
Nuts ✔
Onions & Garlic ✔
Yeast ✔

Nutrients per serving (when recipe serves 12):
Calories: 220
Protein: 3 grams
Fat: 4 grams
Carbohydrate: 43 grams

In saucepan, bring syrup and water to boil. Remove from heat and add butter. Set aside.

In large bowl, mix together flour, sugar, baking powder, and salt. Add egg, milk, and shortening to make batter. Pour into greased 8-inch (2 L) square pan.

Pour maple syrup sauce slowly over batter. Sprinkle coconut on top. Bake in 350°F (180°C) oven for 35 minutes or until tester inserted in center comes out clean. Let cool. Serve with whipped cream.

Make 8 to 12 servings.

Cranberry Carrot Cake with Cream Cheese Frosting

Nutrients per serving
(when recipe serves 16):
Calories: 551
Protein: 6 grams
Fat: 27 grams
Carbohydrate: 71 grams

The cranberries in this recipe add a subtle tartness to this perennial favorite.

1-½ cups	granulated sugar	375 mL
1 cup	vegetable or canola oil	250 mL
5	eggs, at room temperature	5
2-½ cups	all purpose flour	625 mL
2-¼ tsp	baking powder	11 mL
2-¼ tsp	cinnamon	11 mL
2 tsp	baking soda	10 mL
1 tsp	salt	5 mL
3 cups	peeled and grated carrots	750 mL
1-½ cups	fresh cranberries	375 mL

In large bowl combine sugar, oil, and eggs.

Add flour, baking powder, cinnamon, baking soda, and salt and mix. Fold in carrots and cranberries. Divide evenly between two 9-inch (2.5 mL) round greased and floured cake pans.

Bake in 300°F (150°C) oven for about 45 minutes or until tester inserted in center comes out clean. Let cakes cool for 5 to 10 minutes in pan before turning out onto racks to cool completely. When cool, frost with Cream Cheese Frosting (recipe follows).

MAKE AHEAD: The Cranberry Carrot Cake can be baked a day in advance, wrapped in plastic wrap or foil, and stored at room temperature until ready to be frosted.

Cream Cheese Frosting

½ cup	unsalted butter, at room temperature (1 stick)	125 mL
8 oz	cream cheese (1 package)	250 g
1 tsp	vanilla	5 mL
4 cups	icing sugar	1 L
¼ tsp	lemon zest	1 mL

Cream together butter, cream cheese, and vanilla until fluffy.

Beat in icing sugar to make smooth and spreadable consistency. Stir in lemon zest. Frost cooled Cranberry Carrot Cake.

Makes 12 to 16 servings.

Crème Brûlée with Rosemary

This traditional French recipe is brought up to date with the addition of fragrant rosemary.

6	egg yolks, at room temperature	6
⅓ cup	granulated sugar	75 mL
2 cups	35% cream	500 mL
½ cup	homogenized milk	125 mL
1 tbsp	chopped fresh rosemary	15 mL
	Additional sugar for caramelizing	

In large stainless steel bowl, mix egg yolks and sugar until well blended.

In heavy saucepan over medium-high heat, bring cream, milk, and rosemary to gentle boil, stirring occasionally. Remove from heat.

Gradually, in steady stream, pour heated cream mixture into egg yolks and sugar while constantly beating with whisk. Allow mixture to sit for 30 minutes at room temperature.

Strain mixture through sieve into ramekins or custard cups. Place ramekins in a roasting pan. Fill pan with boiling water so that it comes half-way up sides of ramekins.

Place *Bain Marie* (roasting pan with water) in 350°F (180°C) oven; bake for 30 minutes. Custard is cooked when thin knife inserted into center of custard comes out clean. Remove ramekins from roasting pan and place in refrigerator to cool, uncovered.

Prior to serving, cover custard in each ramekin with generous layer of granulated sugar. Caramelize by placing ramekins on baking sheet under preheated broiler. Watch carefully and remove once sugar has caramelized into rich amber color.

Makes 4 servings.

This recipe is FREE of the following triggers (marked ✔)

Caffeine ✔
Chocolate ✔
Citrus fruits ✔
Red wine ✔
Aged cheese ✔
MSG & Nitrates ✔
Aspartame ✔
Nuts ✔
Onions & Garlic ✔
Yeast ✔

Nutrients per serving:
Calories: 580
Protein: 8 grams
Fat: 52 grams
Carbohydrate: 20 grams

Moltoff with Fresh Berry Compote

Nutrients per serving (when recipe serves 10):
Calories: 399
Protein: 5 grams
Fat: 3 grams
Carbohydrate: 88 grams

This fantastically light and elegant dessert will leave your guests clamoring for more!

Caramel Moltoff

3 cups	granulated sugar	750 mL
1 cup	water	250 mL
10	egg whites	10
1 tsp	baking powder	5 mL
2 tbsp	unsalted butter	25 mL
1 cup	water for water bath	250 mL
1 to 1-½ cups	vanilla custard	250 to 375 mL

In small saucepan over moderate heat, melt 2 cups (500 mL) sugar, stirring until darkened in color. Add 1 cup (250 mL) water and let reduce to syrup stage. Do not allow to reduce too much. Caramel should not be too dark. Caramel should thicken slightly as it cools.

In bowl, beat egg whites with remaining sugar and baking powder until soft peaks form. Add 1 tbsp (15 mL) of caramel and continue beating to incorporate. Set aside remaining caramel for serving time.

Butter inside of chilled round angel cake tube pan and fill with egg white mixture. Place filled pan in deep baking or roasting pan filled with boiling water. Make sure water comes halfway up side of angel cake tube pan.

Bake in 375°F (190°C) oven for 10 to 14 minutes or until golden brown. Remove from oven and water bath and let cool to room temperature. Invert onto rack and remove from pan.

Fresh Berry Compote

1 cup	water	250 mL
2 cups	granulated sugar	500 mL
2 tbsp	orange liqueur (optional)	25 mL
2 cups	each fresh blueberries, raspberries, and strawberries	500 mL
	Icing sugar	

MAKE AHEAD: The moltoff, caramel, and berry compote can all be made a day in advance. Refrigerate overnight and bring to room temperature before serving.

In saucepan over medium-high heat, bring water, sugar, and orange liqueur (if using) to boil. Simmer until mixture becomes syrup. Add berries and remove from heat. Let cool to room temperature.

Reheat remaining caramel. Slice moltoff into sections and place on individual dessert plates with base of vanilla custard. Top with berry compote and drizzle with reheated caramel. Dust edge of each plate with some icing sugar sifted through sieve or fine strainer.

Makes 8 to 10 servings.

Lemon Curd with Shortbread Cookies and Raspberry Coulis

Nutrients per serving (when recipe serves 8):
Calories: 494
Protein: 5 grams
Fat: 26 grams
Carbohydrate: 60 grams

The sweetness of the shortbread and the raspberries is matched with the zesty taste of lemon in this delectable recipe.

Lemon Curd

4	egg yolks, at room temperature	4
½ cup	granulated sugar	125 mL
⅓ cup	fresh lemon juice	75 mL
¼ cup	unsalted butter, at room temperature	50 mL
Pinch	salt	Pinch
2 tsp	lemon zest	10 mL

In saucepan, whisk egg yolks and sugar together.

Add lemon juice, butter, and salt.

Cook over medium-low heat, stirring constantly until mixture has thickened. Do not boil.

Place zest into heat-resistant bowl. Place strainer on top and pour egg mixture through strainer. Throw out what remains in strainer.

Allow curd to cool. Store in covered jar in refrigerator if not using right away.

Raspberry Coulis

½ cup	water	125 mL
1 tbsp	cornstarch	15 mL
1	pkg (about 15 oz/425 g) frozen, sweetened raspberries	1

In bowl, mix water and cornstarch together.

In saucepan, simmer raspberries over medium heat until all frost is gone; quickly bring to boil. Pour in cornstarch and water mixture, stirring constantly.

Cook for 1 minute, stirring constantly. Don't cook too long or it will turn brown.

Remove from heat and let cool.

Shortbread Cookies

1-½ cups	unsalted butter, at room temperature	375 mL
½ cup	granulated sugar	125 mL
4 cups	all-purpose flour, sifted 3 times	1 L

In mixing bowl, combine butter and sugar and beat until very light and fluffy.

Place on work surface and knead in all flour, a little at a time. On lightly floured surface, form dough into flattened disc and then roll out to ¼-inch (5 mm) thickness.

Cut into shapes about 4 inches (10 cm) in diameter. Gather scraps, re-roll, and cut into as many cookies as possible.

Place cookies on cookie sheet lined with parchment paper. Bake in 350°F (180°C) oven for approximately 10 to 12 minutes or until lightly golden in color. Transfer to rack to cool.

Place cookie on individual plate. Drape 1 tbsp (15 mL) of lemon curd over portion of cookie. Add portion of raspberry coulis over curd. Garnish with scattering of fresh raspberries or blueberries.

Makes 6 to 8 servings.

MAKE AHEAD: Lemon curd can be prepared a day in advance; raspberry coulis can be prepared several days in advance; and shortbread cookies can be baked a day or two in advance. Store them individually in airtight containers in the refrigerator.

Mocha Mousse with Cinnamon Whipped Cream

Nutrients per serving:
Calories: 420
Protein: 5 grams
Fat: 32 grams
Carbohydrate: 28 grams

This rich dessert is quickly assembled. It contains decaffeinated espresso, but, even "decaffeinated" coffees contain small amounts of caffeine.

5	eggs, at room temperature, separated	5
1 cup	granulated sugar	250 mL
½ cup	unsalted butter, melted (1 stick)	125 mL
¾ cup	decaffeinated espresso (or instant)	175 mL
2 cups	35% cream, whipped until stiff	500 mL

In bowl placed over pan of simmering water, or on top of double boiler over simmering water, beat egg yolks and sugar. Add butter and whisk to combine. Continue to cook, whisking constantly, for 6 to 8 minutes or until mixture is thick, like custard. Don't overcook eggs or allow water to boil or eggs will curdle.

Remove from heat and stir in espresso. Cool to room temperature.

In large bowl, beat egg whites until thick and fluffy and stiff peaks form. Gently fold egg whites into whipped cream.

Stir about ⅓ egg-cream mixture thoroughly into cooled coffee mixture. Fold remaining egg-cream mixture into coffee mixture until thoroughly blended.

Pour into 8 dessert dishes or martini glasses. Chill for several hours. Serve with dollop of Cinnamon Whipped Cream (recipe follows).

MAKE AHEAD: The Mocha Mousse can be made earlier in the day and chilled for several hours.

Cinnamon Whipped Cream

3 tbsp	granulated sugar	50 mL
1 tsp	cinnamon	5 mL
1 cup	35% cream	250 mL

In small bowl, mix sugar and cinnamon together.

In large chilled bowl, whip cream until frothy. Add sugar mixture and whip until medium stiff peaks form. Serve dollops on top of mocha mousse.

Makes 8 servings.

Whole Wheat Doughnuts

The whole wheat flour in these doughnuts adds a nice texture. They're great for dunking in coffee or tea.

2-½ cups	all-purpose flour	625 mL
2-½ cups	whole wheat flour	625 mL
2 tsp	each baking soda, baking powder, and cream of tartar	10 mL
3	eggs	3
1-½ cups	granulated sugar	375 mL
1 tsp	vanilla	5 mL
1 tsp	nutmeg	5 mL
1 tsp	salt	5 mL
½ tsp	ginger	2 mL
¼ cup	butter	50 mL
1-½ cups	milk	375 mL
	Shortening or vegetable oil for frying	
	Sugar and cinnamon for rolling (optional)	

This recipe is FREE of the following triggers (marked ✔)

Caffeine ✔
Chocolate ✔
Citrus fruits ✔
Red wine ✔
Aged cheese ✔
MSG & Nitrates ✔
Aspartame ✔
Nuts ✔
Onions & Garlic ✔
Yeast ✔

Nutrients per serving:
Calories: 211
Protein: 2 grams
Fat: 15 grams
Carbohydrate: 17 grams

In large bowl, mix together flours, baking soda, baking powder, and cream of tartar. Set aside.

In another large bowl, beat together eggs, sugar, vanilla, nutmeg, salt, and ginger until thick.

Melt butter and add to milk. Add milk mixture alternately with flour mixture to egg mixture, beating after each addition just until blended.

Cover dough and refrigerate for 2 to 3 hours or overnight.

Roll out on floured board to ½-inch (1 cm) thickness. Cut with floured doughnut cutter. Deep fry at 375°F (190°C) until golden brown on both sides. Drain on paper towel. Roll in sugar and cinnamon mixture.

Makes about 4 dozen doughnuts.

Carob Chip Cookies

Nutrients per serving:
Calories: 63
Protein: 1 gram
Fat: 3 grams
Carbohydrate: 8 grams

If chocolate is a trigger, try these delectable carob chip cookies. Kids—and adults—love them.

1-⅔ cups	all-purpose flour	400 mL
2 tsp	baking powder	10 mL
½ tsp	baking soda	2 mL
½ tsp	salt	2 mL
⅔ cup	brown sugar	150 mL
½ cup	margarine	125 mL
1	egg	1
⅓ cup	corn syrup	75 mL
1 tsp	vanilla (optional)	5 mL
1 cup	carob chips	250 mL

In mixing bowl, sift together flour, baking powder, baking soda, and salt.

In another bowl, cream together sugar, margarine, egg, corn syrup, and vanilla (if using). Add sifted dry ingredients to creamed mixture. Add carob chips and mix gently with your fingers.

Drop by small teaspoon (5 mL) well apart on greased cookie sheet. Bake in 350°F (180°C) oven for 10 to 12 minutes or until golden brown. Cool on cookie sheet for a few minutes, then remove to racks to cool completely.

Makes about 60 cookies.

No-Bake Carob-Oatmeal Macaroons

These yummy treats can be ready in less than 15 minutes.

2 cups	granulated sugar	500 mL
½ cup	shortening	125 mL
½ cup	carob powder	125 mL
½ cup	milk (or milk substitute)	125 mL
3 cups	rolled oats	750 mL
½ cup	shredded coconut or raisins	125 mL

In large saucepan, mix sugar, shortening, carob powder, and milk. Boil mixture until it bubbles.

Remove from heat and add oats and coconut (or raisins). Mix well and drop by tablespoonfuls (15 mL) onto cookie sheets covered with waxed paper.

Makes about 2 to 3 dozen.

This recipe is FREE of the following triggers (marked ✔)

Caffeine ✔
Chocolate ✔
Citrus fruits ✔
Red wine ✔
Aged cheese ✔
MSG & Nitrates ✔
Aspartame ✔
Nuts ✔
Onions & Garlic ✔
Yeast ✔

Nutrients per serving
(1 macaroon when recipe
makes 3 dozen):
Calories: 112
Protein: 1 gram
Fat: 4 grams
Carbohydrate: 18 grams

Almond Crescents

Nutrients per serving:
Calories: 64
Protein: 1 gram
Fat: 4 grams
Carbohydrate: 6 grams

These crescent-shaped treats have the mellow flavor of almonds and icing sugar. They're perfect with herbal tea.

2-¼ cups	flour	550 mL
½ tsp	salt	2 mL
1-¼ cups	softened butter	300 mL
1 cup	icing sugar	250 mL
2 tsp	vanilla	10 mL
1 cup	ground almonds	250 mL

In bowl, stir together flour and salt. In separate bowl, cream butter; beat in sugar and vanilla. Gradually add dry ingredients to creamed mixture. Add almonds.

Form into 1-inch (2.5 cm) balls; shape into crescents. Bake on ungreased cookie sheet in 325°F (160°C) oven for 12 to 15 minutes or until lightly browned. Sprinkle with icing sugar while still warm.

Makes about 6 dozen cookies.

Icebox Ginger Snaps

Memories of childhood will abound when the warm and wonderful aroma of baking ginger snaps fills your kitchen.

1 cup	shortening	250 mL
2/3 cup	molasses	150 mL
1/3 cup	brown sugar	75 mL
3 cups	all-purpose flour	750 mL
2 tsp	ginger	10 mL
1 tsp	cinnamon	5 mL
1/2 tsp	salt	2 mL
1/2 tsp	baking soda	2 mL
1/2 tsp	cloves	2 mL

This recipe is FREE of the following triggers (marked ✔)

Caffeine ✔
Chocolate ✔
Citrus fruits ✔
Red wine ✔
Aged cheese ✔
MSG & Nitrates ✔
Aspartame ✔
Nuts ✔
Onions & Garlic ✔
Yeast ✔

In bowl, cream together shortening, molasses, and brown sugar. In separate bowl, mix flour, ginger, cinnamon, salt, baking soda, and cloves. Add to creamed mixture. Shape dough into roll 2 inches (5 cm) in diameter. Wrap in waxed paper and refrigerate until firm, about 4 hours.

Cut dough into 1/4-inch (5 mm) slices. Bake on greased baking sheet in 400°F (200°C) oven for 5 to 7 minutes or until lightly browned. Let cool for a few minutes on baking sheets; transfer to racks to cool completely.

Makes about 5 dozen cookies.

Nutrients per serving:
Calories: 72
Protein: 1 gram
Fat: 4 grams
Carbohydrate: 8 grams

Beverages

Mint Julep

On a warm summer's evening, this traditional southern beverage's tangy/sweet flavor is the perfect refresher. Substitute apple juice for the lemon juice if citrus is a trigger.

1	bunch fresh mint	1
1-½ cups	sugar	375 mL
1 cup	lemon juice	250 mL
½ cup	water	125 mL
3 pints	ginger ale	1.5 L

Discard stems and injured leaves of mint. In bowl, cover good leaves with sugar, juice, and water. Let stand 30 minutes. Pour over ice in large pitcher. Add ginger ale.

Makes 10 servings.

Nutrients per serving:
Calories: 176
Carbohydrate: 44 grams

Peppermint Cooler

This frosty beverage is excellent served as a dessert. It's rich in calcium, too!

8 cups	milk	2 L
½ cup	sugar	125 mL
1 tsp	peppermint extract (or more to taste)	5 mL
	Vanilla ice cream	
	Peppermint stick candy, crushed	
	Mint leaves	

In large saucepan, heat milk and sugar until sugar is dissolved. Let cool and chill.

When chilled, add peppermint extract. To serve, place scoop of vanilla ice cream in tall glass and pour milk mixture over it. Garnish with crushed peppermint candy and mint leaf.

Makes about 8 servings.

This recipe is FREE of the following triggers (marked ✔)

Caffeine ✔
Chocolate ✔
Citrus fruits ✔
Red wine ✔
Aged cheese ✔
MSG & Nitrates ✔
Aspartame ✔
Nuts ✔
Onions & Garlic ✔
Yeast ✔

Nutrients per serving:
Calories: 261
Protein: 10 grams
Fat: 9 grams
Carbohydrate: 35 grams

Migraine Mellower

This recipe is FREE of the following triggers (marked ✔)

Caffeine ✔
Chocolate ✔
Citrus fruits ✔
Red wine ✔
Aged cheese ✔
MSG & Nitrates ✔
Aspartame ✔
Nuts ✔
Onions & Garlic ✔
Yeast ✔

Nutrients per serving:
Calories: 80
Carbohydrate: 20 grams

A soothing beverage with the medicinal attributes of ginger.

⅓ cup	apple juice	75 mL
½ cup	ginger ale or ginger beer	125 mL

In tall glass, combine apple juice and ginger ale. Garnish with thin slice of candied ginger, if desired.

Makes 1 serving.

Frosty Fruit Punch

Try making a frozen version of this punch. Your children will love this delicious slushy treat.

1	can (355 mL) frozen unsweetened apple juice concentrate	1
1-½ cups	unsweetened grape juice	375 mL
¼ to ½ cup	fresh squeezed lemon juice	50 to 125 mL
¼ cup	cranberry juice concentrate (optional)	50 mL

This recipe is FREE of the following triggers (marked ✔)

Caffeine ✔
Chocolate ✔
Citrus fruits
Red wine ✔
Aged cheese ✔
MSG & Nitrates ✔
Aspartame ✔
Nuts ✔
Onions & Garlic ✔
Yeast ✔

BASE:

Combine apple juice concentrate, grape juice, lemon juice, and cranberry juice concentrate if using.

To make "punch," add 1 can (355 mL) of club soda to 1 cup (250 mL) of punch base.

KITCHEN POINTER: **To use as a frozen drink in a child's lunch, substitute water for club soda. A 6 oz (156 mL) plastic container of this mixture can be frozen and added to your child's lunch box. It will keep the lunch cool and be ready to drink by lunch time.**

Nutrients per serving (1 cup/250 ml):
Calories: 120
Carbohydrate: 30 grams

Hot Spiced Punch

**Nutrients per serving
(1 cup/250 ml):**
Calories: 172
Carbohydrate: 43 grams

In winter, welcome guests with this special warming drink.

2 cups	cranberry juice	500 mL
8 cups	apple juice	2 L
2	cinnamon sticks	2
6	whole cloves	6
½ cup	brown sugar	125 mL

Place spices and sugar in percolator basket and pour juices into pot. Percolate for 5 minutes. May also be simmered on stovetop.

Makes 10 servings.

Mulled Cider

This old-fashioned favorite is perfect for a festive holiday gathering or wintry night with the family.

1	large apple	1
20	cloves	20
4 cups	apple juice or apple cider	1 L
½	whole nutmeg	½
5	short cinnamon sticks (4 for garnish)	5
1 tsp	ground ginger	5 mL
¾ cup	brown sugar	175 mL

Stud apple with cloves. Place in pot. Pour in apple juice. Break nutmeg and one cinnamon stick. Add along with ginger to pot. Simmer for 30 minutes. Add sugar. Strain into mug. Garnish each mug with cinnamon stick and slice of apple.

Makes 4 servings.

This recipe is FREE of the following triggers (marked ✔)

Caffeine ✔
Chocolate ✔
Citrus fruits ✔
Red wine ✔
Aged cheese ✔
MSG & Nitrates ✔
Aspartame ✔
Nuts ✔
Onions & Garlic ✔
Yeast ✔

Nutrients per serving:
Calories: 280
Carbohydrate: 70 grams

Bibliography

Bickerstaff, E.R. *Neurological complications of oral contraceptives*. Oxford: Clarendon Press, 1975.

Bousser M.G., and H. Massiou. "Migraine in the reproductive cycle." In J. Olesen et al, *The Headaches*. New York: Raven Press, 1993.

Critchley, Macdonald. "Migraine: From Cappadocia to Queen Square," in *Background to Migraine* (ed.) Robert Smith. New York: Springer-Verlag, 1967.

Edmeads, John. "History of migraine treatment." *Can. J Clin Pharmacol* 1999; 6 (suppl A), Autumn: 5A–8A.

Edmeads J., H. Findlay, P. Tugwell et al. "Impact of migraine and tension-type headache on life-style, consulting behaviour, and medication use: a Canadian population survey." *Can. J Neurol Sci* 1993; 20:131–137.

Epstein, M.T., J.M. Hockaday, and T.D. Hockaday. "Migraine and reproductive hormones throughout the menstrual cycle." *The Lancet* 1975; 1(7906):543–548.

Ferrari, M.D. The Economic Burden of Migraine to Society. *Pharmacoeconomics* 1998; 13:667–676.

Gilmour, H. and K. Wilkins. *Statistics Canada, Health Reports 2001*; Vol. 12, No. 2. Catalogue 82-003.

Goadsby, Peter et al. *Headache in Clinical Practice*, Oxford: Isis Medical Media Ltd., 1998.

Hu, X.H., et al. "Burden of Migraine in the United States: Disability and Economic Costs." *Archives of International Medicine 1999*; 159: 813-818.

Kudrow, L. "The relationship of headache frequency to hormone use in migraine." *Headache* 1975; 15 (Apr):36–40.

Lipton R.B., and W.F. Stewart. "Migraine in the United States: Epidemiology and Health Care Use." *Neurology* 1993; 43 (suppl 3):6–10.

McKim, A. Elizabeth. "Ancient Migraine." *Headlines* 8-3, 1999: 1–5.

O'Brien, B., R. Goeree, and D. Streiner. "Prevalence of Migraine Headache in Canada: A Population-Based Survey." *Int J Epidemiol* 1994; 23:1020–1026.

Osterhaus J.T., R.J. Townsend, B. Gandek et al. "Measuring the functional status and well-being of patients with migraine headache." *Headache* 1994; 34:337–343.

Pryse-Phillips W., H. Findlay, P. Tugwell, et al. "A Canadian Population Survey on the Clinical, Epidemiologic and Societal Impact of Migraine and Tension-Type Headache." *Can J Neurol Sci* 1992; 19:333–339.

Silberstein S.D. "Migraine and women: The link between headache and hormones." *Postgraduate Medicine* 1995; 97(4):147–153.

Silberstein S.D., and R.B. Lipton. "Headache epidemiology: Emphasis on migraine." *Neurology Clinics* 1996; 14:421–434.

Simon, Maurice (ed.) *The Babylonian Talmud: Seder Nashim* Vol. 3. London: Soncino, 1936.

South, Valerie. *Migraine.* Toronto: Key Porter Books, 1994.

Stewart W.F., R.B. Lipton, et al. "Prevalence of migraine headache in the United States: Relation to age, income, race and other socio-demographic factors." *JAMA* 1992; 267(1):64–69.

List of Resources

World Headache Alliance

More than 40 headache organizations from over 30 nations worldwide have recently come together to form the unprecedented global co-operative World Headache Alliance.

The Alliance aims to improve the lives of people with headache throughout the world by sharing information among existing headache organizations and by fostering the development of new headache organizations in areas where none currently exists. Together, these organizations seek to increase the awareness and understanding of headache as a public health concern with profound social and economic impact.

World Headache Alliance (WHA) member organizations are working side by side with the best headache researchers, scientists, and clinicians today. WHA is working closely with the professionally based International Headache Society (www.i-h-s.org) toward jointly fostering relationships with the World Health Organization in Geneva, Switzerland, in order to ensure that headache disorders receive full attention worldwide.

For up-to-the-minute information, check out the World Headache Alliance's website at www.ihaveaheadache.com. For more information on WHA, you can also contact:

World Headache Alliance
208 Lexington Road
Oakville, ON
Canada L6H 6L6
(905) 257-6229   Fax: (905) 257-6239

Lay (Patient-based) Migraine Organizations
Canada
The Migraine Association of Canada
365 Bloor St. East, Suite 1912
Toronto, ON M2W 3L4
(416) 920-4916 Fax: (416) 920-3677
Toll-free (membership information): 1-800-663-3557
24-hour recorded information: (416) 920-4917
E-mail: support@migraine.ca www.migraine.ca

An important step in managing migraine involves keeping abreast of current developments in migraine treatment and research. It is also important for migraine sufferers to band together in sharing information and in promoting awareness of the serious nature of migraine. Sufferers can look to The Migraine Association of Canada for this assistance. Founded in 1974 by Rosemary Dudley, The Migraine Association is the only national charity solely committed to providing quality services and programs to millions of Canadians afflicted with migraine.

Through The Migraine Association's educational literature, millions learn about this medical disorder, and learn ways of gaining the upper hand in the struggle against migraine's debilitating symptoms. Members of the association receive a comprehensive information package upon enrollment, along with a yearly subscription to the association's newsletter. Information contained in the quarterly newsletter will appeal to both the newly diagnosed and the experienced migraineur. Details on the latest in migraine research, theories, and treatment options are included. Members share victories and failures in their treatment strategies, as well as tips on coping with migraine. Books and videos are sold through the association as well.

The Migraine Association of Canada's awareness events ensure that migraine is recognized as a serious medical disorder. Improved understanding of migraine spawns new interest in medical research; the mobilization of funds for the development of new treatments; and an improved concern for migraine sufferers from doctors, other health-care professionals, government, the media, and the general public.

Fondation Québécoise de la Migraine et des Céphalées
(Quebec Migraine and Headache Foundation)
1575 boulevard Henri Bourassa W., Suite 240
Montreal, PQ H3M 3A9
(514) 331-8207 Fax: (514) 331-8809
E-mail: tete@fqmc.qc.ca www.fqmc.qc.ca
(Service mainly in French, but English-language
brochures available)

Help for Headaches
647 Ouellette Avenue, Suite #104
Windsor, ON N9A 4J4
(519) 252-3727 Fax: (519) 252-5537
E-mail: brent@headache-help.org www.headache-help.org

United States
The American Council for Headache Education (ACHE)
19 Mantua Road
Mount Royal, NJ 08061
(856) 423-0258 Fax: (856) 423-0082
Toll-Free: 1-800-255-ACHE
E-mail: achehq@talley.com www.achenet.org

The American Council for Headache Education is a nonprofit partnership of patients and health professionals, dedicated to advancing the treatment and management of headache and to raising public awareness of headache as a valid, biologically based illness. ACHE's goal is to help sufferers gain more control over all aspects of their lives—medical, social, and economic. ACHE members receive the quarterly newsletter *Headache* as well as free access to an expanding series of brochures, videos, and books covering a wide variety of topics relating to headache. ACHE has established a growing national network of headache support groups, and it has gone on-line, giving members expanded access to headache information and support via Prodigy, America OnLine, and the Internet.

ACHE is affiliated with the American Headache Society (AHS), an organization of more than a thousand physicians, allied with health professionals and research scientists. If you are not already receiving proper medical care for your headache, ACHE can supply you with a complete list of affiliated AHS physician members in your area. An Access to Care Committee has also been founded, to explore problems encountered by sufferers attempting to obtain specialized services and medications.

MAGNUM, The National Migraine Association
113 South Saint Asaph Street
Suite 100
Alexandria, Va 22414-3119
(703) 739-9384 Fax: (703) 739-2342
E-mail: magnumnonprofit@hotmail.com
www.migraines.org

Migraine Association of the Upper Midwest, Inc.
1911 Ryan West
Roseville, Mn 55113
(651) 636-2564 Fax: (651) 636-0663
E-mail: pkirbyrsvle@uswest.net

National Headache Foundation
5252 North Western Avenue
Chicago, IL 60625
(312) 878-7715 Toll-free: 1-800-843-2256
www.headaches.org

Websites

American Academy of Neurology (AAN): www.aan.com
Canadian Medical Association Journal: www.cma.ca/cmaj
Neurology (journal of AAN): www.neurology.org
Ronda's Migraine Page: www.migrainepage.com/
JAMA Migraine: www.ama-assn.org/special/migraine/migraine
Women's Health Interactive:
www.womens-health.com/health_centre/headache/migraine.html

Index